STRIKE CRAFT

STRIKE CRAFT

ANTONY PRESTON

BISON BOOKS LIMITED

First published in 1982 by
Bison Books Inc.
17 Sherwood Place,
Greenwich, CT 06830, USA.

ISBN 0-86124-068-5

Printed in Hong Kong

CONTENTS

6

THE GIANT KILLERS

Just over a century ago the safe and secure world of the big warship, the battleship and the cruiser, was threatened by the small torpedo boat. Today navies feel equally threatened by small missile boats and the wheel has turned full circle.

To understand how it all started we must go back to 1864, when a British engineer, Robert Whitehead, working for an Austrian engineering company was approached by an elderly retired Army officer, Captain Giovanni Luppis. It appeared that he had an invention for attacking ships, a small 'mobile spar torpedo' or explosive charge which could be steered by two wires. The spar torpedo, a weapon which had been proven in the recent American Civil War, was a canister of guncotton mounted on a pole over the bows of a small steam launch. The spar torpedo had sunk two ironclads and damaged a third during the Civil War, but it had one great drawback: its success virtually guaranteed the destruction of the attacker.

Clearly the invention of Captain Luppis promised an improvement over the spar torpedo and Whitehead was sufficiently impressed to make a model, but he subsequently decided that it would not work. However his fertile brain came up with a much better idea, an 'automobile torpedo' which could detonate below a ship's water-line. By 1866 the prototype was ready, a cylindrical vessel driven by a compressed air engine for 300 yards at 6½

knots. Little else is known about the weapon as Whitehead had cannily kept all the details to himself, confiding only in his 12-year old son and an elderly workman.

Two years later Whitehead produced two new models, with improved depth-keeping, capable of running at about seven knots for 700 yards. The Austro-Hungarian Navy showed a lot of interest but had no money to spare, but when British officers saw the trials at Fiume in 1869 they recommended that Whitehead be invited to England to demonstrate his torpedo to the Admiralty. Following exhaustive trials a year later the Royal Navy bought the rights to manufacture the 'Whitehead torpedo,' followed by a series of torpedo boats.

The lead was given by the British boatbuilder John Thornycroft, who adapted the design of his fast steam launches to the new weapon. In 1877 his Chiswick boatyard delivered HMS *Lightning*, the first seagoing boat to be armed with the Whitehead torpedo, but she was closely followed by the French

The steam yacht *Turbinia* was a floating test bed for the Parsons steam turbine. Her success showed the way towards higher speeds for all ships towards the end of the 19th century.

Torpilleur No. 1. By the early 1880s all the leading navies had invested in large numbers of torpedo boats, some of them little more than wooden launches for harbor defense, but others were capable of making long voyages. The French in particular put their faith in the torpedo boat as a weapon to offset the vast superiority of the Royal Navy, deploying large numbers around the Channel ports. It was widely believed that these torpedo boats would be able to force their way into harbors and sink even the most powerful battleships with impunity and many influential commentators prophesied the end of the big ship.

There were however drawbacks to the torpedo boat which prevented it from achieving such success. The light reciprocating steam engines were liable to break down frequently, while their thin steel hulls proved very fragile. To achieve the high speed necessary to overhaul big ships the engines were running at maximum revolutions and the hulls had to be kept narrow, while the silhouette was kept low to avoid being seen at night, all requirements which aggravated their inherent faults.

Although the torpedo boat was by and large a failure, there was no doubt about the ability of the torpedo to sink a ship if it hit, and so torpedo-carrying warships continued to be built. For a while the trend was towards bigger ships, resulting in the torpedo boat destroyer, but as soon as the lightweight internal combustion engine was available thoughts turned once again to producing small torpedo-craft. In 1904 the first 'motor' torpedo boat appeared, a private design built by Comte Recepe; it had a 14-inch torpedo-tube built into the bow. Two years later the Italian FIAT company went one better with a multi-purpose motor boat, armed with a 47mm gun, two machine guns and two 14-inch torpedo-tubes. Her twin 80hp gasoline engines drove her at 16 knots and after successful trials the Italian Navy bought her.

The British firm of Thornycrofts, having pioneered the steam torpedo boat, was naturally interested in finding a successor. The *Dragonfly* could make 18 knots on her single 120hp engine and launched a single 14-inch torpedo sideways, using a folding discharge-chute. The US Navy looked at ways of equipping battleships with steam torpedo boats, but when the craft turned out to be too heavy for the battleships' boat-cranes the motor torpedo boat was seen as the only alternative. The engineer A T Chester produced a novel design in which the torpedo was dropped through a hatch in the keel, but in spite of this the idea

Above: Captain Luigi Rizzo was responsible for one of the major strike craft successes of World War II when *MAS.15* torpedoed and sank the Austro-Hungarian battleship *Szent Istvan* in June 1918.
Below: An Italian MAS-boat of the series MAS.204-217 running trials in 1918. They could be easily converted to MGB's by the addition of a 57mm gun as shown here.

of motor torpedo boats was not pursued. The problem was that the internal combustion engine was not yet sufficiently developed to permit big, reliable units, and so size had to be kept down. This in turn suggested that the true role of small torpedo craft would be to be transported aboard larger warships. This resulted in a number of unsatisfactory compromises between power and size, a problem exacerbated by the fact that the torpedo was a very heavy weapon.

In peacetime no navy can afford the large sums needed to invest in unproven craft such as motor torpedo boats and so none of these experiments bore fruit. But there was another force capable of pushing the design of hulls and engines forward. Since the 1890s the sport of motor boat racing had gained ground. Like powerboat racing today, it was a rich man's sport offering more excitement than traditional yachting. As early as 1900 a gasoline-engined boat won the International Motor Boat Show race in Paris and three years later Lord Harmsworth established the British International Trophy for motor boat racing.

The influence of competition showed in a steady improvement in hull forms, resulting in higher and higher speeds. The first stepped planing hull, the French *Rapiere III*, was built in 1908 and two years later the English *Miranda IV* from Thornycrofts reached the remarkable speed of 35 knots. The German Lürssen yard, on the other hand, developed round-bilge hulls and their boat won the two top championships in 1911.

The years before World War I saw the paradox of the disappearance of the traditional torpedo boat but the failure of the motor torpedo boat to take its place. And yet, as we have seen, giant strides had been taken in the design of fast hulls, and these developments were all to have their effect much sooner than anyone expected.

Shortly before entering World War I the Italian Navy sounded out various firms to obtain designs for motor torpedo boats and prudently enquired about American gasoline engines. By March 1915 it was possible to place an order with the Societá Veneziana Automobili Navali (SVAN) for two 15-meter boats driven by gasoline engines on two shafts, capable of 30 knots and armed with two 18-inch torpedoes. They were christened Motorbarca Armata SVAN o Silurante (SVAN torpedo-armed motor boats) and numbered *MAS.1* and *MAS.2*. On trials they were not an outstanding success, largely because extra weight added

during construction had slowed them down and because the method of launching the torpedoes over the stern was clumsy. However this did not stop the Italian Navy from forming a national volunteer corps, the Corpe Nazionale Voluntari Metonauti (CNVM), although *MAS.1* and *MAS.2* were rearmed with guns in November 1915 and were demoted to submarine chasers.

Before the two prototypes were complete the Navy ordered 20 more boats, *MAS.3* to *MAS.22*, from SVAN. Once again speed proved disappointing, for additional weight brought the maximum smooth-water speed down to as little as 21 knots. But this did not deter the Navy from pushing ahead with plans to use them offensively in the Adriatic. *MAS.5* and *MAS.7* were fitted with 14-inch torpedoes and dropping gear, much like the old torpedo boats and on the night of 6/7 September 1916 attacked Austrian shipping lying off Durazzo (Dubrovnik). The attack was a success and the two MAS-boats escaped after sinking the small steamer *Lokrum*. The enemy had been taken completely by surprise despite the noise made by the gasoline engines.

The solution to the noise problem was to provide electric motors for the approach and *MAS.20* and *MAS.21* were modified in September 1916. On the night of 1/2 November *MAS.20* and two larger warships approached the boom at Pola (Pula) and the tiny craft managed to get across the nets without being sighted. Unfortunately the battleship she was trying to attack had already left the anchorage and after a search lasting two hours all she could find was the old harbor defence ship *Mars*. It was clearly not her lucky night for both torpedoes were caught in anti-torpedo nets, but *MAS.20* still managed to get back safely through the gap in the boom.

The first major success was scored by *MAS.9* and *MAS.13* on 9/10 December, when Captain Luigi Rizzo took them into the roadstead off Trieste to attack the battleships *Wien* and *Budapest*. These two old ships had been a thorn in the side of the Italians because of their persistent bombardments of shore positions and this was not the first attempt to sink them. This time all went well and both MAS-boats got within 200 meters without being detected, after cutting through three 2½-inch hawsers with hydraulic shears. Both *MAS.9*'s torpedoes hit the *Wien* amidships and the old battleship rolled over and sank a few minutes later. The other boat's torpedoes missed the target, but

once again both assailants were able to creep away unseen in the confusion.

All the time the MAS operators were perfecting their tactics. Groups of two or three boats were towed by larger torpedo boats and destroyers to the area of operations, thus saving fuel and providing some protection *en route*. The destroyers could also provide covering fire if the defense tried to put off their retreat. Smoke floats were introduced to make it harder for the defenders to fire at the MAS-boats during the withdrawal. The biggest nuisance was aircraft, particularly the big Austro-Hungarian seaplanes, and on one occasion one of them succeeded in re-capturing a motor boat from *MAS.19* off Trieste.

Once convinced of the value of MAS-boats, the Italians threw themselves energetically into the task of building hundreds. Other firms joined SVAN in the hunt for higher speed and heavier armament. Orlando of Liverno produced the first design for an interchangeable motor torpedo boat/gunboat, *MAS.91* in January 1917; she was armed with two 18-inch torpedoes or a 47mm quick-firing gun, but most important, speed was increased to 27 knots. The American Elco type was also imported and by 1918 the Baglietto-built *MAS.397* boat had exceeded 28 knots. When the Armistice was signed in November 1918 over 400 boats were in service or under construction.

Undoubtedly the finest hour of the MAS-boats was the sinking

Below: The Baglietto-built 'D' Type MAS-boats 397-400 were capable of 28 knots, a speed which rose to 33 knots when armament was reduced.

of the dreadnought battleship *Szent Istvan*, an event known the world over because it was the earliest motion picture sequence of a big ship sinking. On 10 June 1918, as the Austro-Hungarian Navy's battleships were steaming off Premuda Island they were attacked by *MAS.15* and *MAS.21* under the command of Luigi Rizzo. The first salvo fired at the *Tegetthoff* missed but *MAS.15* hit the next astern, the *Szent Istvan*, twice. As the flooding spread unchecked the 22,000-ton ship slowly listed to starboard. Her consorts tried to take her in tow and strenuous efforts were made to save her, but after two-and-a-half hours she gave up the struggle and capsized, hundreds of sailors scrambling over the giant keel. It was a convincing demonstration of the power of the motor torpedo boat and to make the victory even more complete the escorting destroyers had not been able to score a hit on the escaping MAS-boats, let alone catch them.

The Italians hoped to develop MAS tactics even further and four months later planned a large-scale raid on Pola. The old battleship *Re Umberto* was to push a large raft equipped with net-cutters and paravanes through the nets and minefields and then as many as 40 MAS-boats would sweep into the inner harbor. Nothing came of this audacious plan as the Austro-Hungarian Empire was now visibly on the point of collapse, but there could be no doubt in the minds of Italian naval planners about the need to continue with development of bigger and better craft.

The Austrians, with neither the resources to develop motor torpedo boats nor the opportunity to use them, were nonetheless aware of their potential and produced a revolutionary craft.

This was the Müller-Thomamühl air-cushion hydroplane, built in 1915 to the design of a young naval officer. Although she carried two 18-inch torpedoes and achieved 32 knots in the same sea-states as the early MAS-boats, the high command decided that she was no use for naval operations. It was a curious decision for the MAS had already shown their potential and only a few months later another inventor, Szombathy, was ordered to develop another design for a hydroplane torpedo boat. It was completed only two months before the Armistice and had no chance to prove itself before the Dual Monarchy crumbled.

The British, having found their surface warships restricted in their freedom of movement by the threat of U-Boats and minefields, turned to other ways of taking the offensive against the German High Seas Fleet. At about the same time as the Italians were looking into the matter, proposals were put forward by young officers at Harwich for carrying small motor torpedo boats in the davits of light cruisers. It was intended that these boats should be dropped outside the Heligoland Bight and then attack at high speed across the minefields. A speed of 30 knots was regarded as the minimum.

The technical problems were considerable. For one thing, the only light power unit capable of developing the power needed was an aero engine, which would need modification before it could be used in a boat. For another, the hull would have to be strong enough to be hoisted up in a cruiser's davits and yet not exceed the 4¼ tons that they could lift. The Royal Navy also stipulated an armament of one 18-inch torpedo, the smallest which could inflict serious damage on a battleship.

Naturally the Admiralty turned to the firms which had been building fast racing craft before the war and it is hardly surprising that John I Thornycroft's proposals won approval. Using the *Miranda IV* as a model, Thornycroft proposed a 'stepped' hull which would plane easily at high speed, reducing drag and damping down the bow wave. After experiments with other means of launching, it was finally decided to launch the torpedo stern-first from a trough in the after part of the boat. At top speed the torpedo would sink underneath before starting up and reaching its correct depth, by which time the boat would have turned away. There was some risk that the torpedo might be damaged by enemy fire or that the torpedo might overrun the boat, but these were regarded as minor objections.

The craft which resulted was called the 40 foot Coastal Motor Boat or CMB, a designation intended to hide its true purpose. The hull was built of American elm, even the frames, and the prototype *CMB.1* made 33¼ knots on trials. The engine was adapted from an aero unit and to save weight reversing gear was omitted. The trials were a great success and a dozen more boats were ordered immediately.

Although experiments were carried out with CMBs hoisted aboard light cruisers this was quickly abandoned and the first operational units were sent to Dunkirk. In any case, the constant demand for better speed, armament and seakeeping was pushing up weight all the time and before long the weight-limit was dropped. In 1917 a much larger 55-foot CMB was built, capable of launching two torpedoes and planing at 40 knots and this was put into quantity production. An even larger 70-footer was under construction at the end of the war, capable of minelaying.

There were plenty of targets for CMBs in the English Channel and off the Flanders coast. In April 1917 four attacked German torpedo boats off Ostend, sinking *G.88*; a second torpedo boat might have been sunk as well, but the torpedo was a 'dud.' On 23 April 1918 a large force of CMBs joined in the attempt to block Zeebrugge and Ostend. Their task was to add to the diversionary effect by laying smokescreens, firing torpedoes at enemy 'targets of opportunity' and even firing mortars at shore positions. In the confusion they were able to do little more than harass the defenders but they escaped without loss.

An unusual engagement took place off the River Ems in August 1918, when a force of six CMBs was attacked by eight German seaplanes. The CMBs fought back, using their machine-guns and trying to throw off the seaplanes' aim by tight turns at high speed, but although they shot down two of their attackers all were badly damaged. Time was to show that aircraft were the deadliest enemy of small craft.

The British attempt to oppose the Russian Revolution in 1919–20 took the Royal Navy into the restricted waters of the Baltic, an ideal operating area for CMBs, and they were also used at Archangel and on the Caspian Sea. They even proved useful as river gunboats, stripped of torpedoes and fitted with bullet-proof plating around the wheelhouse and extra machine-guns. The biggest operation was however a daring raid on the Soviet ships in Kronstadt, the heavily defended base outside Leningrad. The idea was generated after a single CMB under Lieutenant Agar had sunk the light cruiser *Oleg* and as a result seven more were sent out to the Gulf of Finland.

On the night of 17/18 August 1919 the seven CMBs entered the North Channel off Kronstadt, timing their arrival to coincide with a bombing raid on the base. Their targets were the battleships *Andrei Pervozvanni* and *Petropavlovsk*, the light cruisers and a submarine depot ship, the *Pamyat Azova*, and any other targets which would immobilize the Baltic Fleet. Although greatly reduced in effectiveness since the Revolution two years earlier, the Russian ships were still a danger to the British light forces operating in the Baltic and Admiral Cowan hoped to neutralise them.

The CMBs approached the harbour in line ahead, engines throttled back to cut down both noise and the bow-wave. Two of the forts opened fire but failed to hit the CMBs as they crept by. The seven boats split into three groups, *Nos. 79, 31* and *88*

leading the main attack, *Nos. 86, 72* and *62* following, and *No. 24* attacking the guardship, the destroyer *Gavriil*. Lieutenant Bremner in *CMB.79* led the attack, heading straight for the *Pamyat Azova*, while Lieutenant Dobson in *CMB.31* attacked the *Petropavlovsk*. Both lots of torpedoes hit their mark; the depot ship listed rapidly to starboard and sank, while the battleship was severely damaged. The CMBs were so close that the officers on the bridge of *CMB.88* were stained yellow by the picric acid in their torpedo's warhead when it hit the other battleship, the *Andrei Pervozvanni*.

So far the attack had been a success, although Lieutenant Dayrell-Reed of *CMB.88* had been shot through the head. But *CMB.24*'s torpedo had passed underneath the *Gavriil* and the destroyer retaliated by blowing her small opponent in half with gunfire. Then *CMB.62* collided with *CMB.79*; the former was entering the harbour and the latter was leaving it. Such was the presence of mind of both COs that Lieutenant Brade kept *CMB.62* at full speed, so that the two boats remained locked together long enough for Bremner in *CMB.79* to fire a demolition charge before jumping clear. *CMB.62* had drawn clear, but she failed to hit the *Gavriil* with her torpedo and was in turn sunk by the destroyer's guns. *CMB.86*'s engines broke down before she entered the harbor and *CMB.72*'s torpedo-firing gear was put out of action by a shell splinter. Unable to fire the torpedo, Lieutenant Bedley broke off his attack but succeeded in towing *CMB.86* to safety.

Despite the loss of two CMBs the attack was a success, for the three ships were out of action – only the dreadnought *Petropavlovsk* was repaired, and the Baltic Fleet was effectively reduced to a handful of destroyers and submarines. Six British officers and nine ratings had been killed, while another three officers and six ratings were taken prisoner.

The German Navy made surprisingly little effort to develop an equivalent to the CMB and the first LM-boats were not ordered until the beginning of 1917. The principal problem was the lack of suitable engines, as the Zeppelin engines used proved less than satisfactory. Another development was the FL-boat, known to the British as a DCB or 'Distance Controlled Boat,' a wire-guided pilotless boat with a large explosive charge in the bows. These were guided from shore, using information provided from an overhead aircraft, to attack the British monitors operating off the Belgian coast. One of these 43-foot craft, *FL.8* was destroyed while attacking the monitor *M.23* in September 1917, but a month later *FL.12* hit HMS *Erebus* full amidships. The big monitor stood up surprisingly well to the 1500lb charge of TNT, but she and all other monitors were later fitted with guard-rails to prevent the DCBs from riding up on top of their 'bulges.' Subsequent attacks by DCBs were not successful, but they showed technical ingenuity a good 20 years ahead of their time.

It might be expected that all the major navies would immediately start building large numbers of motor torpedo boats. They had after all just demonstrated that they were a deadly and cost-effective means of waging war, needing only further refinement of engines and hulls to exploit their capabilities. Instead the opposite happened and few navies showed any interest in them. The British allowed their CMBs to be disposed of, the Americans made no attempt to create even the nucleus of a force, and it was left to the Italians to continue experiments. The reasons for this were mainly financial, but the main cause was their very simplicity and cheapness; it was felt that a force of motor torpedo boats could be recreated in a short space of time, just as the British and Italians had in 1915–16.

Time was to show how wrong this was. It takes time to perfect the right sort of engines and, like weapons and tactics, they must be developed at sea rather than on the drawing board. It is significant that the German Navy which paid the most attention to engine-development, entered World War II with the most

Above left: Luigi Rizzo's *MAS.15* being hauled out of the water at Ancona after she had torpedoed the battleship *Szent Istvan*.
Below: By the 1930s the specialist Italian shipyards were producing the '500' series MAS boats which could reach 47–50 knots.

successful designs of all. Similarly the Italians produced a most successful petrol engine and showed the way to more advanced hull-forms. The real problem for the major navies was that the money and manpower available during times of financial retrenchment did not stretch to cover what were seen as 'luxuries.' Small strike craft may be cheap to build, but they require large investments in research and development and large numbers of skilled manpower to operate.

The German Navy on the other hand was hamstrung by the Treaty of Versailles and looked on the motor torpedo boat as a means of making up for the weakness of the Fleet. At first in secret and later more openly, designs were tested to establish a good hull-form and by 1928 it was clear that Lürssen's designs were the basis for development, being both robust and seaworthy. It was also necessary to find a good engine and so development contracts were given to the leading firms, MAN and Daimler-Benz, to produce a reliable high-speed diesel. Once this was achieved the new *Schnellboot* could truly be regarded as the first satisfactory small fast torpedo boat. Although not as fast as the planing craft still favoured in other countries, she had more endurance and could face the rough weather encountered in the Baltic and the North Sea.

The Royal Navy gave no such lead to British industry, but this did not stop the British Power Boat Company and Vosper from building their own craft. Finally in 1936 the first MTBs or Motor Torpedo Boats were ordered, marking the rebirth of Coastal Forces. But the Admiralty had left it too late and the lack of a suitable British engine meant that Isotta-Fraschini petrol engines had to be imported from Italy. Although powerful aero-engines were available, there was no equivalent of the German Daimler-Benz V-20 diesel.

The French had virtually ignored the motor torpedo boat in 1914–18 and had done little beyond building a handful of prototypes, known as VTAs and VTBs (*Vedette Torpille* Type A and Type B), to distinguish small boats from large. More of the larger VTB type were ordered from 1930 onwards, but like the British, designers were hampered by the lack of suitable engines. There was however considerable cooperation with British firms and performance was steadily improved.

As the victims of the 1919 Kronstadt attack, the Russians were very impressed by the potential of the motor torpedo boat. Using the wreck of a CMB from Kronstadt and another captured in the Caspian, the distinguished aircraft designer Andrei Tupolev was able to produce an effective design known as the G5. They were years ahead of their time in having Duralumin hulls for lightness, but this caused severe corrosion.

The US Navy tried to make up for its neglect by launching a public competition in 1937, calling upon designers and builders to submit designs for small craft, including wood- or metal-hulled 60 to 70-feet torpedo boats. The winning designs, a 60-footer by Hewey and Nevins Inc and a 70-footer from Sparkman & Stevens, were immediately ordered, six hulls with various engines. To compare performance two official Bureau of Ships designs were also ordered and the British Power Boat 70-footer which had been bought by the Electric Boat Company (Elco) was also purchased. In spite of political pressure to support US industry the Navy went ahead with an order for 23 of the British design from Elco. Although originally referred to as Motor Torpedo Boats, these craft were given a designation which would become famous: Patrol Torpedo Boats, or PT-Boats.

It is surprising to find that the Japanese, who took such a pride in building powerful and unorthodox warships, should have shown little interest in developing MTBs. Perhaps in their case the strategic emphasis on a major fleet battle blinded them to the potential of strike craft. Maybe they felt, like the Americans, that the vast distances of the Pacific were not suited to small craft, but whatever the reason very little was done. Only in 1939 did the Imperial Navy order an experimental MAS-type from Italy and the six MTBs developed from this design did not enter service until after Pearl Harbor.

Significantly the smaller navies favored the MTB, usually because their geography lent itself to ambush tactics and because big warships were a drain on their slender resources. Much the same reasoning led small navies to acquire steam torpedo boats 50 years earlier; countries like Sweden and Yugoslavia can hide light craft behind the screen of islands along their coasts and indulge in hit-and-run tactics.

The real problem which lay ahead was not one of material, but one of tactics. The truth was that every navy which possessed motor torpedo boats had ideas about their worth, by no means all of them valid. In the words of a senior British officer, 'Very few people knew much about coastal forces and very few had any idea of what they were going to do.' A handful of dedicated specialists thought that they would be able to do almost anything, but the majority looked on them as nothing more than toys. But on one issue almost all were united, to build a lot of MTBs would cost too much money and as a result all too few had been ordered.

Above: Hundreds of sailors abandon ship as one of the *Szent Istvan*'s sisters stands by to rescue survivors.
Below: The dramatic moment as the 20,000-ton *Szent Istvan* rolls over after being torpedoed by *MAS.15*.

E-BOAT ALLEY

The German Navy's *Schnellboote* soon found employment in the North Sea and the English Channel. Until the fall of France in June 1940 there were French coastal convoys and of course the British moved much of their heavy cargo such as coal by means of coasters. To the British the German motor torpedo boats were known as E-Boats and the East Coast convoy route was known as 'E-Boat Alley.' Any night that was calm and moonless was likely to bring an attack from these sleek, menacing craft and if the lookouts and gunners were not alert the attackers would get away undamaged.

In one of these confused encounters *S.31* torpedoed the British destroyer *Kelly*, captained by Lord Louis Mountbatten. The Allied evacuation from Dunkirk should have given the S-Boats their greatest opportunity, but surprisingly they only hit the French destroyers *Jaguar*, *Cyclone* and *Sirocco* and the British destroyer *Wakeful*, sinking three out of the four. The collapse of France brought the S-Boats closer to the English coast and before long the casualty lists began to grow. Nor were the attackers limited to using their torpedoes, for the S-Boat was ideal for clandestine minelaying, with eight magnetic or acoustic mines stowed on the after deck.

As more S-Boats became available the weight of attacks was stepped up. As an example of what could be done, on the night of 25/26 July 1940 six S-Boats attacked a Channel convoy in conjunction with aircraft. After the convoy and its escort had been badly shot up, the S-Boats left their base at Boulogne and sank three ships, in addition to seven already sunk by the bombers. The destruction of this convoy forced the Admiralty to suspend the Channel convoys for a while, proof of how dangerous the S-Boats could be when used correctly.

The Admiralty for its part reacted as promptly as it could by expanding Coastal Forces as soon as possible. The first MTB base on the East Coast opened in January 1940 and by the time that Coastal Forces were officially established as a separate command in November that year three more had been set up. After June 1940 the supply of Isotta-Fraschini engines dried up, but it proved possible to obtain supercharged Hall-Scott engines from the USA and so the building programme was not delayed. An innovation was the Motor Gun Boat, a similar hull to the MTB but heavily armed with guns to provide a greater volume of fire for the defense of convoys.

When the flotillas were up to strength it was at last possible to take the offensive and on 8 September 1940 two MTBs scored the first British success, an ammunition ship sunk and a cargo ship damaged, off Ostend. But until mid-1941 the bigger and better-armed S-Boats generally had the better of such exchanges. Nor

Above: *PT.212* entering a dry dock on the north coast of Sardinia in May 1944.
Below: PT Boats were active during the D-Day landings in Normandy. Here *PT.509* stands by the sinking minesweeper USS *Tide* off Omaha Beach.

Above: *MTB.538*, a convertible prototype built by Vosper. Here she is armed as an MTB with four 18-inch torpedo tubes and twin power-operated 20mm gun.

could the British MTBs and MGBs achieve the sort of spectacular sinkings notched up by their German counterparts, for there was a much smaller volume of coastwise shipping in Europe.

All the while tactics were being learned. Apart from a handful of prewar specialists the majority of S-Boat and Coastal Forces personnel were wartime volunteers new to the job. The prewar image of dashing in at high speed, firing torpedoes at a line of dreadnoughts and getting away scot-free was largely to blame for the amateurish way in which many attacks were made. The first lesson was that torpedoes had to be fired at relatively slow speed, or else they dived straight to the bottom. Next, torpedoes had to be fired at fairly close range; if fired at a mile or more the torpedo would probably miss or its wake would be spotted by the enemy. But the worst problem was noise, for if the approach was made at high speed enemy lookouts were bound to spot the MTB before she was within range. The S-Boat was better in this respect for the Daimler-Benz diesel discharged its exhaust underwater and for British MTBs the solution was to creep in on a quiet auxiliary engine. The main virtue of high speed was to enable the attackers to break away rapidly after the engagement, rather than in attack. Another tactic developed was to lie

Below: *MTB.48* was built by J Samuel White in 1940. Her three Sterling gasoline engines gave her a speed of 39 knots.
Below right: *S.128* was one of the wartime German 'E Boats.' They differed from the earlier *Schnellboote* in having an enclosed forecastle.

in wait ahead of a convoy, with engines shut down, while MGBs were often used to engage the convoy's defenders, allowing the MTBs to approach from a different quarter undetected.

Whatever tactics were used these encounters were brief, hair-raising and frequently bloody. An attack called for split-second judgement and iron nerve and once battle began it was an affair of multicolored tracers flying in all directions, punctuated by explosions. The petrol-engined boats were liable to catch fire and blow up from a single tracer bullet and this respect the diesel-driven S-boat had another advantage. Many new weapons were developed specifically to deal with S-Boats, notably the 'Headache' gear for monitoring radio messages and rapid-firing guns for destroyers. Royal Navy destroyers in 'E-Boat Alley' were given a light 'bowchaser' gun right up on the forecastle and later a twin 57mm mounting was developed.

What is remarkable is that even as late as June 1941 there were only four flotillas of S-Boats operating in the North Sea, some 25 boats. Yet during the first six months of that year they were able to sink 16 merchant ships totalling 28,000 tons. There were so few S-Boats that when Hitler decided to invade Russia three out of the four flotillas had to be withdrawn to support German operations in the Baltic.

The pattern of operations was repeated, starting with an audacious mine-laying operation in the eastern Baltic on the night that Operation 'Barbarossa' was launched. For a while the S-Boats had things their own way, but poor cooperation with the Luftwaffe robbed them of greater successes. Finally after only two months the Kriegsmarine decided, probably rightly, that other areas were more important to the German war-effort; two flotillas returned to the North Sea while one went to the Black Sea and the other to the Mediterranean. Surprisingly the

Above *S.18* was one of the last of the German prototypes for war production. She was followed by the S.38 type.

Baltic operations had shown up several weaknesses in the design of S-Boats, particularly minor technical faults which tended to put the whole boat out of action. One of the flotillas, for example, had no more than five or six operational boats out of a total strength of ten.

A new flotilla was formed to serve in the Arctic from October 1941, with a view to hindering any British attempt to send supplies to north Russia and to attack Soviet shipping off Murmansk. The operation was plagued by bad luck, one of the S-Boats running aground and two more colliding with one another. With only two craft operational little could be achieved, and reinforcements did not arrive until the following summer. Even that did not improve matters and apart from a series of mine-laying trips to the Kola Inlet the flotilla was inactive. Their

problem was the long Arctic summer twilight, which robbed them of the ability to operate under cover of darkness for most of the summer. Nor did the end of summer allieviate matters as the onset of autumn was certain to produce weather too bad for extended operations. Finally the flotilla was disbanded in July 1942, having been wasted in a basically hostile environment.

The growing number of S-Boats coming forward from the ship-yards enabled more effort to be put into the North Sea and Channel areas in the early months of 1942. But the British were getting the measure of S-Boat countermeasures, and they too had plenty of reinforcements. The basic Vosper 70-footer was

Below left: *MTB.238*, a Vosper 72½-footer, was armed with two 21-inch torpedoes, a 20mm gun and twin .5-inch machine guns.
Below: *MGB.510* was an experimental type armed with a 6-pdr (57mm) gun, two twin machine guns and two 18-inch torpedo tubes.

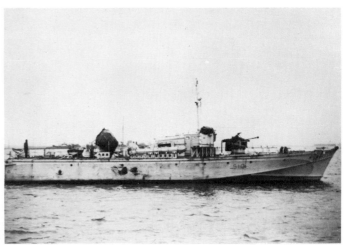

Above: One of the original Vosper 70-footers, *MTB.34*, returning home after an active night in the Channel.

Above right: The British Power Boat-built MGBs 107-176 were reclassified as MTBs and renumbered in 1943. *MTB.449* however has still to receive her two 18-inch torpedo tubes.

enlarged and fitted with new weapons and some of the US Navy's Elco type PT-Boats were made available under Lend-Lease. Radar was now available, not only to the aircraft of Coastal Command but to Coastal Forces, and this enabled more interceptions to be made. The result was a series of fierce actions fought to establish mastery.

Two actions demonstrate the nature of this struggle. The first was fought in July 1942, when seven S-Boats set out from Cherbourg to attack shipping passing through Lyme Bay. Early on the morning of 8 July the flotilla found its quarry, a long line of merchantmen escorted by armed trawlers, and the S-Boats immediately fanned out into an attacking formation. On silenced diesels, four approached to within 500 yards before their main engines burst into life with a shattering roar. The four S-Boats leapt forward like greyhounds loosed from the leash and eight torpedoes sped away towards the enemy. In the confusion it was impossible to tell which boat hit which ship, but the defending fire was wild and as the attackers turned away to reload their torpedo-tubes the remaining three roared into a second attack. The result of this catastrophic action was

six ships sunk, four cargo ships, a tanker and one of the escorting trawlers.

In contrast Coastal Forces had warning of a sortie by R-Boats (the German equivalent of MGBs) from Calais on the night of 16 August. Two MGBs were already at sea and they were joined by three more from Dover; both groups were ordered to join forces in mid-Channel and attack the German force, now known to include at least 20 R-Boats. When they came upon a group of six R-Boats the British force opened fire first at a range of less than 100 yards, damaging them severely. *MGB.330*, with nearly all guns out of action, rammed an R-Boat deliberately and sank her. The other four MGBs continued firing at the enemy, hitting several and setting them on fire. From German survivors it was later learned that the MGBs had sunk two R-Boats outright and damaged another so severely that it had to be abandoned. In addition two more were badly damaged and the action marked a clear victory for the British.

On the opposite side of the Channel the German convoys were having considerable success in running the gauntlet until early in 1942. The 'Channel Dash' by the battlecruisers *Scharnhorst*

Above: *MTB.376* leaves war-damaged Grand Harbour, Malta.
Above right: *MTB.476*, an ex-MGB, is armed with a 6-pdr gun and
two 18-inch torpedo tubes.
Below: *MTB.80*, a Vosper 72½-footer at speed, showing the hardchine
hull lifting clear of the water.

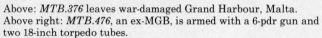

and *Gneisenau* in February 1942 is well known, but what is often forgotten is the part played by MTBs and S-Boats. The battlecruisers' screen included a strong force of S-Boats and R-Boats, which succeeded in beating off an attack by five MTBs from Dover, one of the last chances the British had of stopping the operation. In March the disguised raider *Michel* succeeded in brushing aside massed attacks by destroyers, MTBs and MGBs, when she made her way from Kiel to Brittany. Yet when the *Stier* made the same run in May her escorting torpedo boats were both sunk.

The British were able to form new flotillas with the large number of craft now available. A novel addition to their strength was a force of Steam Gunboats, virtually small destroyers capable of reinforcing the MTBs and MGBs. Initially known by SGB-numbers, they were given the names *Grey Goose*, *Grey Owl*, *Grey Shark* etc, under which they achieved considerable renown. The SGB Flotilla was taken over by Lt-Cdr Peter Scott, who brought a new dash and vigor in the handling of coastal forces. Another addition to the strength was a new type of long-hulled craft, the Fairmile 'D.' Here at last was a craft with sea-worthiness to match the S-Boat, although the petrol engine was still a weak point. These 'Dog-boats' were capable of functioning as MGBs or MTBs, according to the needs of the moment, a major advance in operational flexibility and of course their larger hulls permitted a heavier scale of armament than the short-hulled boats.

Far left: The Fairmile 'B' Type Motor Launches (MLs) performed a useful support task. Over 500 were built.
Center left: *MTB.422* passes wrecked shipping in Livorno. She was one of five American 'Higgins' Type PT.Boats made over to the Royal Navy under Lend-Lease.
Near left: A Vosper 73-footer, *MTB.381*. This flush-decked design carried an armament of four 18-inch torpedo tubes, a 20mm gun and six machine guns.

Another factor contributing to Coastal Forces' growing dominance over the S-Boats was air power. As the Allied air forces gained mastery in the air over the Channel, it became more and more hazardous for German light craft. The equipment and tactics which had already begun to end the freedom of the U-Boats to recharge their batteries on the surface at night could equally be used against craft moving under cover of darkness. Radar was now available in sufficient quantity to allow both Coastal Forces and RAF Coastal Command to be properly equipped with the latest surface search radars.

There was a final ingredient: better training. When Commander Peter Dickens took command of the 21st MTB Flotilla he realised that part of the problem for Coastal Forces was a lack of coherent tactical thought. He pioneered the concept of the unhurried approach, like a hunter stalking his quarry, and began to analyse results in a way which had not been done before. An example of his tactical innovation was the procedure to be followed if a force of MTBs or MGBs was sighted; one craft would start firing and maneuvering at high speed, drawing enemy fire and allowing the others to approach quietly from a different direction. If the remainder was sighted the decoy then slowed down in turn and started to make a silent attack.

The combination of Dickens' torpedo tactics and MGB tactics developed by the other great Coastal Forces leader, Robert Hichens, proved the key. When they finally worked together as respective Senior Officers of the MTB and MGB flotillas at Felixstowe, tactics could be worked out jointly and although Hichens was subsequently killed the procedures which he had refined with Dickens became standard for Coastal Forces.

As Coastal Forces grew in strength and confidence their area of operations was extended. During the winter of 1942 a force of Norwegian-manned MTBs began to raid shipping in Norwegian waters and landed Commandos. These operations were carried out with the new 'Dog-boats,' which also began to operate off the coast of Holland with considerable success.

In contrast the S-Boats' position deteriorated throughout 1943. Although the German Navy had been keen to develop S-Boats as a means of attacking British shipping in 1940, it had not occurred to the Naval Command that its own coastwise shipping would ultimately come under attack. The disruption of the iron ore imports through Rotterdam forced the Germans to send much of the traffic through Emden in river-barges, imposing a severe strain on an already overloaded canal-system. Both Spain and Sweden were becoming reluctant to charter merchant ships for the iron ore trade with Germany and this forced the Third Reich to use its own scarce mercantile tonnage.

It would be wrong however to talk of the S-Boats having been defeated. In the autumn of 1943 they switched to new tactics, using the maximum number of boats for one large sortie, rather than attacking in small numbers over a wide area. At the end of September three flotillas attacked a convoy off Harwich and a month later no fewer than 28 S-Boats launched a massed attack from Ijmuiden against a convoy off Cromer. It was later estimated that the battle which ensued broke down into 16 separate actions, as the S-Boats vainly tried to penetrate the convoy's defenses. When dawn came the British had lost an escorting trawler and the Germans had lost two S-Boats but the convoy was unharmed.

Left: *MTB.447* and her sisters had three Packard gasoline engines developing 4050hp, producing a smooth water speed of 39 knots.

Above: One of the early Vosper 70-footers *MTB.23* firing her torpedoes
at speed. Wartime experience however showed that torpedoes must be
launched at low speed to prevent them diving too deep.
Below: *MTB.297* returning to port at full speed after she and *MTB.228*
had torpedoed the old cruiser *Niobe* (formerly *Dalmacija*) in the
Adriatic in December 1943.

Another innovation was to adopt direct attacks. Instead of relying on silence the S-Boats now took to attacking at high speed, hoping to out-distance the escorting destroyers. It could also be unwise to pursue a fleeing S-Boat too far, for they had a trick of luring a pursuer almost to the Dutch coast and then turning on him.

During the build-up before the Normandy invasion in June 1944 emphasis switched back to the English Channel. For the first time a force of American PT-Boats was used in Northern European waters, but they were intended primarily for 'cloak and dagger' operations rather than attacks on German shipping. However for D-Day itself three PT-Boat squadrons were employed to guard the flanks of the beachhead. With their Allied counterparts they joined in a series of fierce night actions, preventing the S-Boats from harassing the huge invasion armada lying off the beaches.

When one remembers that there were literally thousands of targets available, the S-Boats' efforts were a dismal failure. During the first week of the invasion they sank only a dozen or so ships and lost three of their own. Air strikes took out four more and then on the night of 14 June a massive bombing raid on Le Havre sank 11 and damaged three, a blow from which the Channel flotillas never recovered.

Right to the end the S-Boats remained dangerous. As late as March 1945 they were able to sink two merchant ships in the Scheldt estuary, while the mines that they laid sank 11 more. Not until Germany itself was crumbling did the S-Boats give up the struggle. At the surrender only 15 boats were still operational – as against over 300 craft in Coastal Forces.

Above left: A Fairmile 'B' Type, *ML.145* carried a variety of weapons and also laid mines.
Left: *MGB.673*, a Fairmile 'D' Type, bristles with guns. These 115-footers were capable of 31 knots.

BATTLE FOR THE MED

In the autumn of 1941 the German Navy, faced with the need to prop up its Italian ally, decided to move an S-Boat flotilla to the Mediterranean. As activity in the Baltic was virtually at an end the 3rd Flotilla was earmarked for the Mediterranean, while the 1st Flotilla was to be sent to the Black Sea to keep up pressure on the Soviet Union.

The journey of the 3rd Flotilla was a minor epic, involving ten S-Boats and all their spares and support equipment moving all the way from the North Sea to the Mediterranean without going through the Straits of Gibraltar. From Rotterdam the flotilla went up the Rhine to Strasbourg, where they transferred to the Rhine-Rhône Canal. Passing through 167 locks and the famous Burgundian Gate, they then traversed the River Doubs and the Saône, finally joining the Rhône at Lyons. Even a S-Boat was a tight fit in the locks on the Rhine-Rhône Canal and it was necessary to use the slightly smaller type, with 16-cylinder engines, to get through the locks.

Security was strictly maintained throughout the operation. The 20mm gun was removed, the torpedo-tubes were covered over with sheet metal and a dummy funnel was built on deck. The wheelhouse had to be cut off to pass underneath the low bridges, and was carried on deck. The Reich Service flag was worn instead of the naval ensign and the crews wore civilian clothes, as the cover-story was that a force of air-sea rescue launches was in transit.

The Flotilla moved in two divisions; the first was operational at Augusta in Sicily by December 1941, while the rest joined them a month later. From Sicily they could harass Malta, laying mines and picking off unwary small craft. In May 1942 they moved to Derna in North Africa, a forward base for attacking the big 'Vigorous' convoy to Malta. During the evening of 14 June they sank the destroyer HMS Hasty and damaged the cruiser Newcastle. They were also able to interdict the evacuation from Tobruk, sinking a minesweeper and several small vessels and even capturing a tank landing craft.

In theory the Italian MAS-boats should have been able to make a considerable nuisance of themselves, even without German reinforcements, for there were some 60 boats operational. But the Type 500 boats were not sufficiently robust and even their weapons were unsatisfactory. Nevertheless they achieved successes, notably the sinking of the cruiser HMS Manchester in August 1941 and the submarine Turbulent in March 1943. In the Red Sea MAS.213 hit and damaged the anti-aircraft cruiser HMS Capetown in April 1941.

Above: *MAS.534* and her sister *MAS.533* in December 1941. The
former was later sunk by German air attack in the Adriatic.
Below: Two Italian Series 500 MAS-boats at high speed. In spite of
their outstanding performance, the MAS failed to achieve many
significant results during World War II.

In spite of their weaknesses the Italian Navy deployed its MTBs wherever the Axis needed reinforcement, even as far afield as Lake Ladoga, outside Leningrad. In January 1942 the Naval Command answered a German request for help by sending MTBs, midget submarines and explosive motor boats to the Black Sea. This called for as much ingenuity as the S-Boats' trip from Germany; they were taken by large road-transporters from Venice to Vienna and from there towed to Galatz. They then made their own way down the Danube, reaching the sea at Constanza before crossing the Black Sea to Yalta in the Crimea. The 19th MAS Flottiglia became operational in May 1942, and three months later scored a major success by blowing the bows off the cruiser *Molotov*.

What could have been the proudest chapter in the story of the MAS turned out to be a disaster. On 26 July 1941 a coordinated attack was planned on Malta, using MAS, midget submarines and aircraft. The plan was audacious, typical of the daredevil temperament which had led the Italians to develop the MAS way back in 1915. The frigate *Diana* led a force consisting of *MAS.451* and *MAS. 452*, each carrying a *Maiale* or 'pig' human torpedo, and eight explosive motor boats. The latter were known as *Barchini Esplosivi*, but had a camouflage designation, *Motoscafi da Turismo Modificati* (modified tourist motorboats or MTM). They were piloted within range of the target and the operator locked the controls before making his escape, or so the rule book said. The British defenders were alerted by their surface radar, so that the coastal artillery was ready for the attack. In spite of that Major Tesei, leading the assault, was able to destroy the boom and it looked as if the attack would succeed. But the attackers did not allow for the detonation blowing up the St Elmo lifting bridge on the breakwater; the wreckage collapsed and stopped the remaining *Barchini* from getting into Grand Harbour. Early next morning the two MAS were caught by RAF fighter-bombers and destroyed, a devastating end to what could have been a shattering blow to the British.

The S-Boats which went to the Black Sea went from Kiel to Hamburg, and then up the Elbe to Dresden. From there they were taken by road-transporters along the autobahn as far as Ingolstadt, where they were once more put afloat on the Danube. For the journey they were stripped to the bare hull and even the engines had to be removed to reduce weight, but even with a delay caused by ice in the Danube the first four boats of the 1st Flotilla were operational in May 1942. They were just in time for the siege of Sevastopol, during which they were able to inflict several casualties.

The work done by the comparatively small number of S-Boats was tremendous, especially as they were heavily outnumbered by Soviet forces. Whereas the Soviet heavy units were handled cautiously, they used light forces aggressively, particularly in support of commando-type operations behind enemy lines. The Russians fought desperately to save the great naval base and fortress of Sevastopol and thereafter there was heavy fighting in the Straits of Kerch and the Sea of Azov. When the German Army broke through to Novorossiisk in September 1942, the Black Sea Fleet's light forces had to help transport men and supplies from Poti to Tuapse in a frantic effort to stem the advance. Losses were heavy, particularly in action with German and Italian light forces.

An outstanding action was the seizure on 10 September 1943 of Novorossiisk by Russian MTBs (known as TKA or *Torpedny Kater*). Three groups of TKA, 26 in all, based on Gelendik were given the task of entering the harbor and capturing a bridgehead for the landing of three army brigades. The Russians later admitted that the operation had been successful but costly, with the loss of five gunboats, eight motor launches and two minesweepers.

The pattern of operations in the English Channel was repeated

Left: Italian MTS boats at sea. These two-man craft carried a short 17.7 inch torpedo in the stem and could travel for a distance of about 120 miles.

as the Soviet air force gradually won air superiority and the navy's MTBs and gunboats were able to defeat their Axis opponents. However Soviet operations were normally characterized by a lack of imagination and there are many examples of the High Command's failure to exploit the potential of their light strike craft. For example, nothing was done to interrupt the German evacuation of Odessa and Nikolaiev, nor was the evacuation of the Crimea an excuse for unleashing the light forces. Instead the emphasis was put on supporting the army, an important role but only one of the functions for which MTBs and MGBs were suited.

In the Mediterranean Axis light forces reached their peak in August 1942 and thereafter their fortunes declined dramatically. The British victory at El Alamein, followed by the 'Torch' landings in Algeria and Morocco, soon led to the destruction of the S-Boats' bases in North Africa. Then came the Allied landings in Sicily, which forced the S-Boats to move from Taranto to Viareggio. Although they succeeded in sinking an American destroyer, the USS *Rowan*, off Salerno, it is interesting to read in German records that the S-Boat flotillas felt that they had been abandoned by the Naval Command. Even so, their discipline and dedication made them formidable opponents. Even when forced to evacuate Taranto in September 1943 one of them laid mines as she left and one of these sank the British minelayer HMS *Abdiel* next day, with heavy loss of life.

Two S-Boats left for the Adriatic and there they managed to wage what amounted to a private war. On 11 September 1943 they sank the Italian gun boat *Aurora* off Ancona and on the same afternoon they captured a troop transport and torpedoed the destroyer *Quintino Sella* south of Venice. By now almost out of fuel, they then persuaded the garrison of Venice to surrender to them, having convinced the Italian defenders that they were supported by dive-bombers and tanks.

In October 1943 two flotillas (11 S-Boats) moved into the Adriatic, having travelled through northern Italy via the River Po. There were rich pickings in the form of numerous small craft running arms and supplies to the Yugoslav partisans and many of them were sunk. Gradually however the process of attrition wore them down to eight boats and when hostilities ended in May 1945 only five were left at Pola. It had been a hard-fought battle.

The British had been able to reinforce the Mediterranean flotillas in the spring and summer of 1943, particularly with the new Fairmile 'D' type. They had been able to make the journey by sea, having been modified to carry extra fuel in deck-tanks. They were joined by American PT-Boats as well, but they suffered from the dearth of targets. This is reflected in the extraordinary variety of subsidiary duties performed by light craft in 1943–44. Only when action flared up in the Adriatic and Aegean did they begin to justify their existence.

An unusual feature of the small-ship combat during this period was the use by both sides of converted landing craft as inshore gunboats. The Germans used F-lighters and the British used their Landing Craft, Gun (LCG) to provide heavy firepower in support of inshore operations. The F-lighter was a particularly doughty opponent when upgunned and armored and its light automatic 37mm and 20mm guns were usually supplemented by 88mm flak guns which could smash a PT-Boat or MTB into matchwood. The American PT-Boats were particularly valuable in these operations because of their superior surface-search radar. They normally provided reconnaissance and targeting information for MTBs and MGBs.

One of the most successful operations was a patrol by three PT-Boats in June 1944, patrolling out of the base at Bastia in Corsica. Between La Spezia and Genoa they picked up what appeared to be two escorts and tracked them for half an hour, running on silenced engines. The three PT-Boats then each fired two torpedoes and turned away, still creeping on silenced engines. Suddenly the leading target blew up, the second started firing wildly and then the radar-screens went blank. Postwar research showed that the six torpedoes had accounted for the small destroyers *TA.26* and *TA.30*, both ex-Italian Navy ships operating under German control. The action encapsulated all the lessons and improvements of wartime experience and lived up to the ideal attack as envisaged by people like Peter Dickens, not only to attack undetected but to leave the scene still undetected.

Below: *MS.15* and other Series I *motosiluranti* were copied from German designs.
Right: *MAS.539* being winched out of the water. The small size of these craft allowed maintenance to be carried out on shore.

PT-BOATS IN THE PACIFIC

Contrary to expectations the new PT-Boats of the US Navy were not hurled into the Pacific War. For a start, events had moved so fast after Pearl Harbor that there hardly was time to get forces moved into the Central Pacific. Another factor was the immense distances covered by the carrier task groups; the big battles of Coral Sea and Midway had been fought well away from land and the rival ships had not even seen one another. Only when the time came to make an amphibious landing would there be any chance to attack Japanese warships on anything like equal terms.

That chance came at last in August 1942 when the far-reaching decision was made to invade the Solomon Islands. The landing planned for Guadalcanal was certain to stir up a hornet's nest and in that sort of close-range fighting the PT-Boat was likely to prove vital. The only PT-Boats in the Pacific were Squadron 2's 14 boats at Panama and these were divided into two squadrons and shipped out to Noumea in New Caledonia as deck-cargo aboard cargo ships.

Left: A PT-Boat escorts landing barges at Nassau Bay, New Guinea, July 1943.
Below: PT-Boats take evasive action under a Japanese air attack during the Leyte Gulf landings, October 1944.

Inevitably the initial attempts to set up a forward base were chaotic. There was great difficulty in getting the 50-ton hulls off the cargo ships for there was no crane available for three weeks. Once afloat the boats had to move with their tender, the converted yacht *Jamestown*, to Tulagi. Their new operational base was only 35 miles across the water from Guadalcanal, where the US Marines were locked in a bloody struggle to stop the vital airstrip from falling into Japanese hands. Night after night Japanese warships came down the 'Slot' from Rabaul to bring in reinforcements of men and ammunition and to bombard the American positions. With their superior training in night-fighting the Japanese had already inflicted severe casualties and it was now absolutely vital that the PT-Boats try to redress the balance.

The crews worked hard to set up their new operating base on 12 and 13 October and the four boats, *PT.38, PT.46, PT.48* and *PT.60*, were ready when at 0200 hours the following morning the alarm sounded. A force of Japanese warships had come down the 'Slot' and were busily bombarding the Marines' position. Intelligence was as poor as the tactical appreciation of what PT-Boats could do – at first, when it was thought that only three destroyers were coming, the PT-Boats' commander thought that they were not sufficiently worthy opponents!

Above: *PT.1* shipped as deck cargo on the seaplane tender USS *Pocomoke*.

Such illusions were shattered as soon as the PT-Boats cleared Tulagi harbor on that moonless night. Apart from the distant flash of gunfire nothing could be seen in the inky blackness and nobody realised that the four boats in line ahead had already passed through a picket line of eight Japanese destroyers. The squadron became separated, with *PT.60* well ahead of *PT.46* and *PT.48*, and *PT.38* several miles away to the east. *PT.60* fired two torpedoes at what she identified as a cruiser and then turned and ran for home, oblivious of the fact that she was running into the destroyers. Two of them gave chase, but were unable to hit the small target and, although she was subsequently damaged on a reef while waiting for a patrolling destroyer to move away, she escaped without further damage.

PT.46 and *PT.48* had a much more frightening time, being illuminated by searchlights and bracketed by heavy shells, but miraculously both escaped. They had however found no targets because, as the reports put it, by the time a Japanese destroyer was sighted the PT-Boat was too close to fire a torpedo. Being so far away, *PT.38* avoided the fire which had been directed at her squadron-mates, but when she tried to fire her torpedoes only one of the four got into the water. Two stuck in the tubes and one damaged its fins by striking the deck as it shot out (the humid air in the Solomons had affected the powder-charge), but the fourth ran straight and apparently exploded. So confused was the whole series of actions that the US Navy was convinced that *PT.60* and *PT.38* had each sunk a cruiser, but postwar research is quite clear that no Japanese warships were hit that night. The problem was one that affected all actions involving small strike craft – from a small bridge only a few feet above the waterline very little can be seen and often torpedoes exploding on hitting the seabed or the seashore were mistaken for hits.

Until the PT-Boats could be fitted with radar they could do very little except harass the Japanese, who proved much more proficient at the deadly game of night-fighting. Even allowing that they caused confusion merely by appearing on the scene, contemporary accounts show that an equal amount of confusion was created among the PT-Boats. In fact, far from being a menace to the bigger warship, PT-Boats proved frighteningly vulnerable to destroyers. In the best-known of such incidents a destroyer cut *PT.109* in half and very nearly put paid to the career of Lieutenant John F Kennedy.

The main target of the PT-Boats' attentions was the famous 'Tokyo Express,' a nightly supply-run from Rabaul to Guadalcanal. It was led by a man widely reckoned to be the finest Japanese commander of World War II, Rear-Admiral Raizo Tanaka. His light cruisers, destroyers and fast transports made their runs as regularly as any express train. For the Japanese it was the only hope of preventing the Americans from gaining a vital foothold in the Solomons and equally for the Americans, 'derailing the Tokyo Express' was given top priority.

For the PT-Boat crews the strain became almost unbearable. Not only were they continually frustrated in their attempts to surprise the Japanese, but also the enervating climate of the Solomons was beginning to wear them down. To be out three nights in four was not uncommon and it was normal for the officers and men to catch a few hours sleep and then to work all day on the engines for the following night. Mechanical faults were inevitable, given the strain the boats were under and it was not unusual for five out of the eight boats at Tulagi to be incapable of going to sea. By December 1942 the efficiency of the squadron was seriously affected by the strain. Most personnel had succumbed to a combination of malaria, dengue and dysentery and were way below the tough mental and physical standard required for operating light strike craft, yet these 'zombies' still managed to show what they could do.

On the night of 9 December *PT.59* and *PT.44* were sent to investigate an intelligence report that a Japanese submarine would be landing men on a clandestine mission. As predicted the submarine was there and *PT.59* was the best placed to fire two torpedoes. They ran true and the *I.3* disappeared in a shower of debris. Although the submarine had been a sitting duck it was heartening to the crews back at Tulagi to know that PT-Boats were as deadly as they had been claimed.

Only two nights later they scored another heartening success, when *PT.37, PT.40* and *PT.48* set up an ambush for the 'Tokyo Express' off Savo Island. They were lucky that the usual clammy haze of the Solomons had given way to a clear night and so, although they had lost visual contact with one another, the lookouts sighted the Japanese first. They slid out into the channel and took up their firing positions and they fired their spreads of torpedoes almost simultaneously. There was a tremendous explosion and this time there was no false claim for they had torpedoed Tanaka's flagship, the big destroyer *Terutsuki*. The raid was abandoned, for Tanaka had been injured by the blast, and after he had been taken off the *Terutsuki* was left to sink and the 'Tokyo Express' headed back to Rabaul. However the Japanese took their revenge, for two PT-Boats ran into Japanese destroyers shortly afterwards. They had inadvertently allowed themselves to be silhouetted against the burning glow of *Terutsuki* and that was sufficient for the alert Japanese lookouts.

Other actions took place once the 'Tokyo Express' started again, but time was running out for the Japanese. The grim war of attrition was finally wearing them down. On 1/2 February 1943 a last big effort was made by the Japanese, but this time the Express was running empty; the Japanese had decided to pull out from Guadalcanal and a light cruiser and 20 destroyers were coming down the 'Slot.' It was a bad night for the PT-Boats, who failed to hit any of the Japanese ships and suffered in return the loss of three of their number.

In retrospect it can be asked what the PT-Boats had achieved off Guadalcanal. The answer is not much in material terms. However it must be remembered that at a time when US destroyers and cruisers were outclassed and outfought by the Japanese,

Above: A PT-Boat firing her 20mm gun and her .5-inch machine guns at Japanese positions on Biak, New Guinea.
Above right: John F Kennedy and the crew of *PT.109* in 1943.

particularly in view of the overwhelming superiority of the 'Long Lance' torpedo, the PT-Boats were virtually immune to torpedoes; They could also strike back and they posed a threat which the Japanese could never ignore. Without the presence of PT-Boats the Japanese could have had much more freedom of action and that might easily have made the difference between victory and defeat.

At about the time that operations in the Solomons were beginning to go against the Japanese another theater of operations was becoming crucial. The successful outcome of the

Battle of the Coral Sea had frustrated a Japanese drive on Port Moresby, the capital of New Guinea, but the Japanese were still in possession of the northern shore and until they were expelled they remained a threat to Australia.

The battle for possession of New Guinea resolved itself into a struggle to dominate the northern shoreline, for the Japanese had a string of garrisons needing resupply from the sea. Here was an ideal target for PT-Boats and early in 1943 a base was established at Tufi. Their targets were the small barges and lighters used to run in ammunition and food, the best-known being the 46ft Daihatsu type, built originally of steel but later of

Below: Weaponry on the deck of *PT.131* includes short 21-inch torpedoes, rocket launchers and a 20mm Oerlikon gun.

wood. They were armored with bullet-proof steel around the bridge and carried a defensive armament of machine guns. What made them an even tougher nut for PT-Boats to crack was that they drew less than three feet of water and torpedoes would run underneath. Being diesel-powered for the most part, they could absorb much heavier punishment than the PT-Boats and they were to prove doughty opponents.

The first detachment at Tufi numbered only six PT-Boats in January 1943, but eventually the New Guinea PT-Boat Command was expanded to 14 squadrons. They used several bases and were supported by eight mobile tenders. The early 'barge-busting' operations showed just how tough the Daihatsu craft were and there was considerable discussion about the best tactics to deal with them. The initial reaction was to use speed, but eventually stealth was shown to be the right approach, as it had in the Solomons and in the English Channel. In March two PT-boats *PT.114* and *PT.129* tried the new ideas out in a daring attack on Mai-Ami Bay, in Huon Gulf, which was suspected of being a barge-terminal. The two PT-Boats arrived in the area after dark, cut engines and waited to see what would happen. Eventually *PT.129* moved out into the Gulf to see what had happened to the enemy, but *PT.114*'s patience was rewarded when they heard the noise of voices and engines. Although it sounds hard to believe, the incessant tropical rain had blanketed the sound to such an extent that two Japanese barges actually bumped into the PT-Boat without realising what she was.

Being so close the .50 inch machine guns could not depress far enough to hit, but Lieutenant Dean ordered submachine guns to be passed around and with these the men of *PT.114* attacked the barge alongside. As the boat pulled away her guns were able to rake the other barge. At this moment *PT.129* returned at high speed and helped to polish off the remaining four barges.

The next step was to 'acquire' 37mm aircraft cannon and one of these was mounted on the bow to provide more firepower. By July the PT-Boats were moving further up the coast in search of new targets and in that month another unusual action was fought. *PT.142* and *PT.149* found themselves in the middle of a convoy of some 30 barges and were even called up by the Japanese with lamp-signals. Their reply was to open fire and in the murderous exchange which followed six barges were sunk and the PT-Boats sustained hits themselves.

The later boats sent out to New Guinea were armed with the new 40mm Bofors gun, a great improvement over the machine

Above: An aerial view of a PT-Boat at speed. The heavy torpedo tubes have given way to Mark XIII short torpedoes.

Above left: PT-Boats of Squadron 1 pass the carrier USS *Hornet* off Pearl Harbor in April 1942.
Left: *PT.14*, an Elco 70-footer, running trials in 1940. She became the Royal Navy's *MTB.263* in 1941.
Below: The Elco built *PT.105* and two sisters on trial. These 80-footers could make 40 knots in smooth water.

Above: PT-Boats of Squadron 13 making their way northwards through the Inland Passage from Seattle to Alaska in 1943.
Below: An Elco PT Boat fires two of her Mark VIII torpedoes during exercises off the Newport Torpedo Station.

guns and 20mm cannon previously used. Bofors guns were scrounged wherever they could be found and it was even felt worthwhile to remove two torpedo tubes to permit the extra weight. Another innovation was to move in closer to the shoreline, where interceptions were much easier to achieve. It meant a great increase in the risks from navigational hazards, for the whole area was studded with uncharted rocks and reefs, but the results justified the gamble. Between July and August 1943 the number of barges sunk rose from nine to 45, clear proof that the PT-Boats were getting it right.

It was normally the rule that a PT-Boat could not survive in daylight under air attack, but in December 1943 *PT.190* and *PT.191* showed how an exception proves the rule. Operating off Arawe in New Britain, they were attacked by an estimated 40 aircraft. There was nothing the PT-Boats could do except zigzag violently and hope that their AA fire would put the Japanese pilots off their aim. The impossible happened; four aircraft were shot down and the remaining attacks became more and more ragged. Even so, sheer weight of numbers might have overcome the PT-Boats had not a group of American P-47 Thunderbolts arrived after forty minutes and put the attackers to flight.

It is hard at this distance to remember just how long it took to clear the Japanese out of the Pacific. 'Barge-busting' in New Guinea was not brought to an end until November 1944, when emphasis shifted to the Philippines. The big base at Mios Wendi was closed down and replaced by a new one at Morotai. From here the PT-Boats were to blockade the 40,000-strong garrison on Halmahera, one of the strongpoints 'leapfrogged' by General MacArthur's island-hopping strategy, but still too dangerous to leave unguarded. Nor was Morotai totally secure, for the Japanese defenders had only been pushed to the other end of the island. The base was kept fully engaged to the end of the war, preventing the garrison on Halmahera from reinforcing their comrades on Morotai.

Top: The remains of *PT.323*, almost bisected by a Japanese aircraft off Leyte, December 1944.
Above: *PT.164* minus her bow after an air attack off Rendova in August 1943.

The real business of the PT-Boats however was to support the big amphibious landings in the Philippines. A day after the landings in Leyte Gulf, 45 boats arrived from New Guinea, having travelled 1200 miles with their tenders. As we know a series of misunderstandings and errors in signalling placed the whole invasion force at risk, with a Japanese decoy force successfully luring away the covering aircraft carriers and leaving only six old battleships to stop a task force heading for Surigao Strait. To support Admiral Jesse B Oldendorf there was a slender force of destroyers and 39 PT-Boats, deployed on either side of the strait. Their most important task was to report on numbers and disposition of the Japanese and only then did they have freedom to attack.

The Japanese were alert and their gun crews had little difficulty in beating back the PT-Boats' attacks. Ten were hit, but only one was sunk. *PT.137* succeeded in damaging the light cruiser *Abukuma* – with a torpedo which underran its original target! *PT.490*, *PT.491* and *PT.493* attacked a destroyer and thought they had scored a hit, but *PT.493* was hit twice by heavy shells and had to be run ashore on a coral reef. Further north *PT.323* helped to finish off the destroyer *Asagumo*, which was dead in the water, near the burning cruiser *Mogami*.

The PT-Boats had played their part in destroying the Imperial Japanese Navy's last surface fleet, but they still had work to do in the Philippines. The Japanese were always resourceful in supplying their outlying garrisons and from their main base

Below: The sleek lines of *PT.140* are shown to advantage in this photograph taken on a training run off Melville, Rhode Island in November 1943.

Above, near right: The crew of *PT.321* haul aboard a waterlogged Japanese survivor in Surigao Strait, October 1944.
Above, far right: *PT.354* mounts a quadruple bazooka armament, a home-grown modification.
Below right: *PT.25*, an Elco 70-footer, is pictured here on her completion.

in Ormoc Bay they were able to feed in small craft carrying supplies and ammunition. Several actions took place between the PT-Boats and the Japanese patrol craft and as late as 12 December a destroyer was sunk. This was the *Uzuki*, torpedoed by *PT.492* and *PT.497* on the west coast of Leyte.

Space does not permit a detailed account of the work done by PT-Boats in the Philippines, but some idea of the scale of operations can be guessed at. By the summer of 1945 the base at Bobon Point, Samar, was operating over 200 PT-Boats and training was starting for the invasion of the Japanese home islands.

It might be thought that the PT-Boat had earned its place in the postwar US Navy, but this was not to be. Out of 212 boats operational in the Philippines in August 1945, no fewer than 118 were immediately surveyed and found to be defective. After being stripped of engines, guns and every useful item of gear they were burned off Samar beach, a sad and undignified end after all they had endured and achieved. Even the boats in the United States were hurriedly disposed of and by 1946 only four new craft were still on the Navy List. Even these were destined to be sold to South Korea in 1952, for the US Navy could see no role for the PT-Boat in warfare dominated by guided missiles and radar. Time was to show how wrong they were.

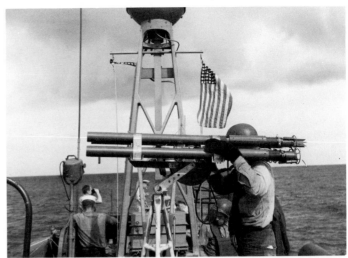

THE FAST PATROL BOATS

For many years after World War II the British retained a lead in strike craft, now given the generic title of fast patrol boats or FPBs. The old distinction between MTBs and MGBs had become blurred, with all new craft being designed for interchangeable guns and torpedoes and even so-called torpedo boats carrying a gun-armament far heavier than anything called an MGB in 1941.

The first change was in propulsion. Recognizing that the weak point of their MTBs and MGBs had been the Packard petrol engine, the British decided to exploit their lead in gas turbines and in 1947 a Camper & Nicholson long-hulled FPB, *MGB.2009* went to sea with a Gatric gas turbine. Considering that she was a leap in the dark, when such problems as blade-fatigue and ingestion of salt water were only dimly understood, *MGB.2009* was surprisingly successful. She was purely experimental and did not serve long, but she showed that both noise and vibration could be controlled, despite the enormous increase in power.

Despite this bold step the 'conventional' FPB continued to be built. The British built two large classes, the Packard-engined 'Gay' class and the diesel-engined 'Dark' class. These could be regarded as the last fling of the old short-hulled designs, being only 75ft long – the 'Gay' class were largely wooden whereas the 'Dark' boats were of composite construction, wood planking on aluminum framing. They were like their wartime predecessors noisy and lively, but they carried the exceptionally heavy armament of four 21-inch torpedo-tubes and a twin 20mm gun as torpedo boats or a 4.5-inch gun and a 40mm Bofors as gunboats.

The 4.5-inch gun, otherwise known as the Coastal Forces Mk 1 or the 4.5-inch 8cwt, looked a formidable weapon but it was only a qualified success. In an attempt to follow the successful wartime 6-pounder (57mm) the Admiralty adapted an Army 114mm low-velocity gun which had originally been intended for the demolition of concrete fortifications. On a modified twin Oerlikon power-mounting it encountered a host of teething troubles, but in spite of these it was issued to Coastal Forces postwar. Having very low velocity and a short barrel the gun lacked range and old Coastal Forces hands swore that you could see the shell leave the muzzle and wobble on its way.

The decision to put diesels in the 'Dark' class was based on experience with two ex-*Schnellboote*, *S.208* and *S.212*, which played an unique role in the postwar world. These had been surrendered at the end of the war and were of understandable interest to the British, but once the trials and evaluation were over another use was found for them. The Cold War was as yet an unknown phrase, the Soviet blockade of West Berlin had started and there was no NATO Alliance to defend Western Europe. What was needed was intelligence about the Soviet Navy in the Baltic and so these two S-Boats, minus armament and manned by ex-*Kriegsmarine* personnel, eavesdropped on Russian movements and maneuvers. Nothing could catch them, which was as well, since the German crews would have been executed as spies. No navy recognized them and they could scarcely hope to be granted prisoner-of-war status. The two boats, numbered *MTB.5208* and *MTB.5212*, were for some years fishery protection craft with the British Rhine Army Flotilla.

Below: HMS *Brave Borderer* was one of the last and also one of the most successful British designs. She was armed with four 21-inch torpedoes and two 40mm guns. Her Proteus gas turbines gave her a speed of 50 knots.

Above: The world's first gas turbine powered fast patrol boat was the experimental *MGB.2009*. It was driven by a Gatric turbine.

Performance was all-important and an exciting new British diesel, the Napier Deltic, was tried out in *No. 5212*. This unusual engine, which is still in production for minehunters, took its name from a delta or triangular arrangement of opposed pistons and triple crankshafts. Each Deltic developed 2500 brake horse-power at 2000 rpm and yet with its reverse gear weighed only 10,500lb. Its power-to-weight ratio of 4.2lbs per hp was the best yet achieved in a marine diesel and had the British not invested so much in gas turbines the Deltic would certainly have been

developed for future fast strike craft. However the success of the Gatric in *MGB.2009* coupled with advances in aero-engines pointed inexorably towards the gas turbine.

The next step was to get more gas turbines to sea for evalua-tion and in 1953 two much larger FPBs were commissioned, the 122-ft long *Bold Pathfinder* and her half-sister *Bold Pioneer*, each driven by a pair of G.2 gas turbines. The opportunity was taken to evaluate hull-forms at the same time. *Bold Pathfinder* trying a round bilge form, while *Bold Pioneer* used the normal hard chine hull-form. With their massive twin funnels set side by side they were impressive craft and were big enough to carry two 4.5-inch guns and a 40mm Bofors or four 21-inch torpedo-tubes and a Bofors gun.

Experience with the Gatric and G.2 showed that the best results would be obtained if a gas turbine was to be specially designed for the marine environment and in 1952 Peter Scott's famous command, HMS *Grey Goose* went into dock for conver-sion. Her steam turbines were replaced by twin RM-60 turbines

Above: *Bold Pathfinder* was powered by G.2 turbines and could mount two 4.5-inch guns or torpedoes.

developing 50 percent more power than her original steam machinery. In her new incarnation she had twin side by side funnels, as in the 'Bold' boats, but she was no more than a floating test bed and after three or four years of intensive (and highly successful) trials she was scrapped in 1957.

Confidence in gas turbines was gaining rapidly and, once the lessons of the largely experimental 'Bold' class had been absorbed, the Vosper yard at Portchester was given a contract for two composite gas turbines FPBs, known as the 'Brave' class. They were to be driven by three 'marinized' versions of the Bristol Proteus gas turbine. As torpedo boats they carried four 21-inch torpedoes, but instead of the conventional tubes they carried side-launching cradles, an arrangement used in some wartime PT-Boats to reduce weight. The gunboat version was to use the so-called Coastal Forces System Mk 2 or CFS2 gun, a massive 3.3-inch (84mm) gun in a stabilized enclosed shield.

The CFS2 gun system was based on the British Army's Centurion tank gun, the 20-pounder. It used stabilization to compensate for the violent motion and, being designed from the start for the task, had none of the faults of the short 4.5-inch gun. In 1954 one was mounted on a rolling platform at Portland Bill and then it went to sea for trials in the *Bold Pioneer*. It proved popular, giving rise to a new unofficial Coastal Forces motto: 'One Round, One Hit' – a boast that could never have been fulfilled in previous MGBs.

The Proteus was equally successful, proving that the noise of a gas turbine was by no means as severe as its critics had claimed. Its lack of vibration was a marked improvement over the Deltic, which had also been shown to be much noisier. But above all the Proteus offered lightness; with its reversing gearbox fitted, its power-to-weight ratio was still only 1.6lbs per hp. Another clear advantage was its lack of bulk, for the 'Braves' had 25 percent more space available in the engine room than a petrol, or diesel-engined FPB.

The *Brave Borderer* and *Brave Swordsman* attracted a lot of attention, achieving as much as 50 knots in smooth conditions. Denmark ordered six very similar craft in 1962, the *Søløven* class, while the new Federal German Navy ordered a single craft, the *Strahl*. But the hard chine hull proved no better suited to the short, steep seas of the Baltic than it had in the 1930s, when Lürssen had perfected the round-bilge form for the *Schnellboote* and no more were built. What also hamstrung the British

effort to sell their FPB designs was the sudden decision in 1957 to abolish Coastal Forces. It was the old argument: in peacetime fast strike craft are too expensive to maintain as they siphon off funds from more important projects. All the experience and expertise built up since 1939 was thus to be thrown away.

The British decision is even harder to comprehend when it is remembered that other navies showed no such doubt about the efficacy of fast strike craft. Norway, for example, had just placed an order for 12 *Nasty* type, a design which was sufficiently interesting to be evaluated by the US Navy. In Germany the famous Lürssen yard was once again in full production, with the first of 32 *Jaguar* class. Of even more significance was the attention that the Soviet Navy was paying to fast strike craft. Class after class was appearing, *P-4*s, *P-6*s, *P-8*s and *P-10*s, all part of the massive Soviet effort to protect inshore waters. They were fairly small craft, ranging from 82ft to 92ft and armed with two torpedo-tubes. The most successful were the *P-6* type, an estimated 400 of which were built from 1953 to 1960 – a staggering total even by wartime standards.

The first break out of the traditional mould was made by the Royal Swedish Navy. Starting with the 250-ton *Plejad* class in 1950, they enlarged the basic hull to allow a much heavier load of weaponry, associated electronic and a more robust hull. On a hull 157ft long the *Plejad* class (built by Lürssen) mounted six 21-inch torpedo-tubes and two 40mm Bofors guns. In the early 1960s the *Spica* class followed, 141-footers with the same torpedo-armament, but a 57mm Bofors automatic gun in a power-operated enclosed turret and radar-assisted fire control. The *Spicas* and their successors, the very similar *Norrköping* class, displace 200 tons and are driven by three Proteus gas turbines developing over 12,000 horsepower. It is no coincidence that the hull was designed by Lürssen and the seakeeping of the *Spicas* is one of their outstanding features.

The Royal Swedish Navy pioneered the use of very fast (60-knot) wire-guided torpedoes for use against surface targets, at a time when opinion elsewhere was turning against the torpedo. But, whereas the British 21-inch Mk 9 travelled at only 35 knots for 14,000 yards, the Swedish Tp 61, with its hydrogen peroxide fuel, could travel 50 percent further at 60 knots. The guidance-wire pays out very rapidly from a spool in the tail of the torpedo and simultaneously from a spool in the torpedo-tube and the thin wire then floats in the water as it has neutral buoyancy. The advantage of wire-guidance is that the torpedo remains under positive guidance all the way, although in its final run-in it may switch to passive homing on propeller-noise.

The newly formed Federal German Navy had the task of preventing Soviet forces from breaking out of the Baltic and this implied a heavy reliance on strike craft. Following the lead given by the Swedes, in 1970 the Federal German Navy started to equip some of its *Jaguar* class with a new wire-guided anti-ship torpedo known as the *Seeaal* or sea-eel. The ten craft converted were now known as the *Zobel* class and they struck an unusual note in having the two 21-inch torpedo-tubes facing aft. This was to allow the FPB to launch her torpedoes while breaking away and reduced the risks involved in turning under fire.

It was left to the Soviet Union to make the first major break-through. From 1959 reports percolated through to the West of a startling development, a standard P-6 MTB hull armed with two large boxes aft, containing guided missiles. Dubbed 'Komar' by NATO, the new strike craft carried two SS-N-2 'Styx' surface-to-surface missiles and were driven at 40 knots by four-shaft diesel engines. There were many drawbacks to the 'Komar,' however. Because the launch-tubes were open at either end the missiles suffered severely from corrosion and with so much

Above left: The British FBP *Gay Archer,* one of the last gasoline-powered short-hulled boats.
Above: The 'Gay' Class was followed by the 'Dark' Class which were diesel-powered.

armament crammed into an 88ft hull they hardly dared venture outside coastal waters.

The Soviet Navy placed great faith in these missile boats. Many were transferred to 'satellite' navies and both Egypt and the Republic of China built their own versions, but they were only an interim solution until properly designed missile-boats could be built. These started to appear in 1960, the famous 'Osa' class, and scores of them have been built. The 131-ft hull has room for four SS-N-2 'Styx' missiles and, instead of the puny twin 25mm guns of the 'Komar,' the 'Osa' has two twin 30mm automatic mountings. The 'Styx,' although crude by today's standards, was a formidable weapon for its time, a small pilot-

Below: Three British postwar fast patrol boats, *FPB.790* (top), *FPB.5008* and *FPB.5009.*

less aircraft armed with an 800lb warhead. The missile flies under the control of an autopilot, probably with the assistance of commands transmitted from the ship, and has an active-radar homing head or an infrared seeker.

Western navies took little notice of the 'Styx' until 1967. Then on 21 October, during the Six-Day War between the Arab States and Israel, it received its baptism of fire. The Israeli destroyer *Eilat*, an elderly ex-British wartime destroyer, was patrolling off Port Said when she was attacked by two Egyptian 'Komars' lying behind the breakwater. The *Eilat* was a sitting duck, patrolling along a straight line and could offer little more than a token defence from her 40mm guns before being hit amidships by three out of the four 'Styxes' fired. She sank rapidly as flooding spread through an enormous hole amidships and a stunned world realized that the navies of the West had absolutely no defense against such an attack, let alone an equivalent missile.

For a while there was something close to panic in naval circles and the *Eilat* affair was even compared to battles like Lissa or Hampton Roads as a milestone in naval history. In fact the action only resembled Lissa in the sense that it also shed very little light on warfare of the future and created its own mythology. For a start the *Eilat*, in a very exposed position patrolling provocatively off a hostile coast, could have been sunk very easily by other means. For another, the *Eilat*'s fire control and armament were so antiquated that she would have been hard put to defend herself against conventional air attack. Compare what happened six years later, when a force of Israeli FPBs slaughtered a force of 'Osas' during the Yom Kippur War without sustaining more than a small shell-hit during the entire engagement. But the successful use of the 'Styx' in the Indo-Pakistan War of 1971 tended to reinforce the missile's reputation, although the Indian Navy admitted afterwards that they had contented themselves with firing at shipping in harbor rather than fighting an engagement at sea.

Although there were many bitter recriminations about the alleged failure of the West to produce an equivalent to the 'Styx,' the short answer is that the need had not previously been evident. There were, for example, many air defence missiles, but with a large number of aircraft carriers in service in NATO there was no specific requirement for more types of anti-shipping weapons. The French had a project on the drawing-board, later to be known as the Exocet or MM-38 (Mer-Mer 38-km) missile and, as soon as the news of the *Eilat* sinking came through, the manufacturers went ahead with development. In 1970 the first firings at sea were carried out by the small patrol craft *La Combattante* and the trials ship *Ile d'Oléron*. The next step came when the Federal German Navy decided to arm its new Type 148 patrol craft with Exocet MM-38 and the Royal Navy bought it for fitting to frigates. This was the sort of endorsement needed, and by 1977 more than 17 navies had placed orders for over a thousand missiles.

The French were not slow to grasp the opportunity. The Israelis had already approached Lürssenwerft in 1965 for six 45-meter craft armed with 40mm guns, but because the Federal German Government did not wish to anger its Arab customers the order was placed with the French shipyard Constructions Mécaniques de Normandie (CMN) at Cherbourg. These boats were called the *Mivtach* class, but became better-known as the *Saar* class when in 1969 five more of them were impounded in France to conform to a sudden arms embargo. Much to the anger of President de Gaulle all five suddenly escaped from Toulon and reached Haifa in January 1970.

The French now produced their own version of the 45-meter hull, a 47-meter design known for security reasons as the *Combattante II*. Despite this it bore no resemblance to the original laminated wood and fiberglass patrol boat and was virtually identical to the *Saar* class in layout and hull-form. The Federal German Navy wished to buy Exocet for its Type 148 FPBs but France would not permit this purchase unless the *Combattante II* hull was used, with French radar *and* the con-

struction of half the order at Cherbourg, rather than at Lürssen's yard. The German Government, anxious not to disturb the *rapprochement* with France, meekly accepted these rather harsh conditions, and *S.41* to *S.60* were delivered between 1972 and 1974.

The *Combattante II* rapidly carved itself a huge slice of the market, and gave its name to a new generic type. Four were sold to Greece, four to Malaysia, and twelve to Iran. The normal armament is a 76mm OTO-Melara Compact dual-purpose gun forward and two pairs of Exocet launchers angled to port and starboard amidships, but the Iranians chose the American Harpoon missile and the Malaysians favor the Swedish 57mm Bofors gun. The need to accommodate more armament led to the development of the 56-meter *Combattante III* series, usually armed with an additional 76mm gun or a twin 40mm aft and light automatic mountings amidships.

Exocet is fired by one man in the control room. When the FPB enters the battle-zone the magnetron of the homing head is warmed up for about a minute. When the radar detects a target the gyroscope in each missile is run up, requiring another half a minute. Once a target is selected the axial gyroscope must also be aligned and beyond this point the sequence is irreversible. The missile fires itself automatically 2 to 5 seconds after the firing button is pressed, its boost-motor ignites and it accelerates to just below the speed of sound in $2\frac{1}{2}$ seconds. The missile climbs to an average height of 100ft, then pitches over into level flight before descending to its cruising height of 50ft. It is now about $2\frac{1}{2}$ miles away and when it reaches its 'search zone' – a circle from which a target ship travelling at 40 knots could not have escaped during the time of flight – the radar homing head switches itself on. The missile now comes down to a height of

Below: The long-hulled *FPB.5036* armed as a gunboat, with two short 4.5-inch guns and a twin power-operated 20mm.

less than 25 ft, becoming a 'seaskimmer' until it hits the target or is detonated by a proximity fuze as it flies overhead.

The Israelis, understandably sobered by the loss of the *Eilat*, lost no time in developing their own shipborne missile. Israel Aircraft Industries was given the task of developing a small missile with a range of 12 miles. Known as Gabriel, it was nominally outranged by the Styx, but it apparently has the benefit of superior technology. All twelve *Saars* were refitted to take Gabriel, some with eight launchers and others with five. The next step was to design a bigger boat to take Gabriel, the 58-meter *Reshef* class. Ten of these magnificent craft have been commissioned since 1973, armed with two 76mm Compact guns and five Gabriel launchers. Now they are receiving the Gabriel Mk 2, which has improved guidance and a range of 22 miles, making them even more potent.

It is however the smaller *Saars* which have the distinction of being the only Western FPBs to have fought a missile engagement. Details are very sketchy but it is known that in October 1973, during the Yom Kippur War, a force of *Saars* encountered a large force of Syrian 'Osas' (reputed to be 14 FPBs) off Latta-kieh. What is known is that at least six Syrian 'Osas' were sunk without more than a shell-hole in one of the Israeli craft. The

Above left: *Gay Bombadier* at speed in 1953, armed with two 21-inch torpedoes and a twin 20mm gun.
Above: *Gay Charioteer* alongside the minesweeper HMS *Marvel* in 1956.

impossible had happened: the 'unbeatable Styx' had been beaten by a missile of half its range.

From various sources it can be deduced that what the Israelis did was to trick the Syrian missile-controllers into firing at long range and too high. This not only caused the 'Styxes' to miss the Israeli boats, but also made them easy to track on radar. The method used was to drop chaff (the metallic strips known in World War II as 'Window') to confuse the tracker head of the missile. Three helicopters flew low over the leading *Saars* and, when the firing of the 'Styxes' was detected, both the helicopters and the FPBs below fired chaff before opening out their respective formations. The missiles were thus seduced into homing onto the biggest radar-image, that created by the floating mass of chaff. The *Saars* were also fitted with the latest jammers and electronic interception and analysis equipment and just how much this helped can only be guessed at. But above all the Israelis had shown that FPBs could hold their own against missile attack and the new weapon had proved itself in battle.

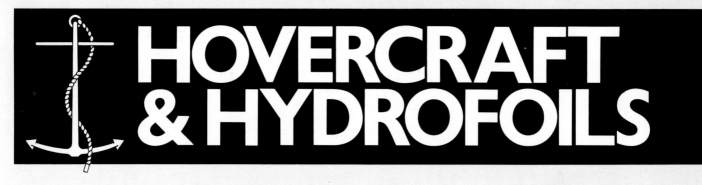

HOVERCRAFT & HYDROFOILS

By the 1960s designers were generally agreed that, however much hull-designs and power units might be improved, there was going to be no significant increase in speeds. If anything, the opposite was true, with a greater emphasis on seakeeping, reliability and robustness, all qualities which are incompatible with ultra-light structures and maximum engine power. Clearly some alternative to the classic 'displacement hull' would have to be developed if the quest for higher speeds was to be pursued.

The answer had already been looked at many years before. In Britain, for example, trials had been carried out on a Canadian design for a ladder hydrofoil as far back as 1921. It was not successful but in 1936 Commander Hampden and the naval shipbuilders J Samuel White produced an 18ft hydrofoil 'runabout.' Although hardly a basis for development, it showed that a hydrofoil, by raising the hull clear of the water, reduced drag to a great extent. The Hampden hydrofoil, on a displacement of 1.34 tons, reached 33 knots, whereas a fast dinghy (1.12 tons) and a fast motor boat (1.78 tons) only reached 24 knots.

The Admiralty was sufficiently impressed by White's proposals for a 67ft hydrofoil MTB to go ahead with an order for *MTB.101* in 1936. She ran her trials in 1940, but the foils and struts produced so much cavitation that she could not get beyond 41.3 knots, no matter how much power was generated. In 1939, the Denny shipyard at Dumbarton put forward a 'semi-hydrofoil' design, using a stepped hull like the old CMBs, but with a single fixed submerged foil at the after end. *MTB.109* was built and on trials in 1944 reached nearly 46 knots. There were however serious practical problems. For one thing it was not possible to fire torpedoes at more than 25 knots and for another, the boat could not turn safely at high speed. The Admiralty reluctantly decided that these faults prevented *MTB.109* from being accepted and so this interesting craft was broken up.

Although much interest had been generated in German research into military hydrofoils, little was done by the British in the postwar years. They had a new toy to play with, the air-cushion craft or hovercraft, which offered a different solution to the problem of drag by floating the hull on a cushion of air inside a rubber skirt. As soon as the hovercraft demonstrated its unique ability to run ashore over a shelving beach, ideas began to churn forth for strike versions armed with guns and missiles and in 1964 came the first mention of a 'hovership' for the Royal Navy.

Sadly none of these dreams came to anything, for although the hovercraft can do what it claims, it does so at much greater cost than any conventional displacement hull. More important it makes much heavier demands on maintenance, a problem already acute for strike craft. In the early 1970s the Shah of Iran ordered six BH.7 hovercraft, four of which were to be armed with surface-to-surface missiles of an unspecified type. This interesting innovation did not materialize however and nobody else has followed this line of development. Not even the Russians, who made a massive investment in military hovercraft in the 1970s, have tried to use them in the strike role, so for the foreseeable future the strike hovercraft can be discounted. One of their biggest drawbacks is noise, which robs them of any element of surprise.

In contrast the hydrofoil has shown remarkable promise. In the 1950s Russian civilian hydrofoil ferries were developed and they were followed by a large number of 50-ton hydrofoil MTBs.

Below: Although not FPBs as such, the fast target boat *Sabre* and her two sisters were the last British fast strike craft. They had two Proteus gas turbines and were similar to the 'Brave' Class.

Top: The Egyptian missile boat *Khyber* leaves Portsmouth for the long voyage to Alexandria. Six of these 52-meter craft have been built in Britain for the Egyptian Navy since 1977.
Above: The Singaporean Navy's FPB *Sovereignty* is armed with a Bofors 76mm gun forward.

51

Above left: The new Thai FPB *Witthayarom*, one of three missile boats built in Italy.
Above: Soviet Osa Type missile boats in line ahead, showing the massive SS-N-2 missiles.
Left: The Turkish FPB *Dogan* was built by Lürssen and armed with eight Harpoon missiles.

Known as the *PA-4* class, they had a bow foil to assist in reducing drag at top speed. They were not particularly successful and were replaced by the *P-8* class in the early 1960s. In the mid-1960s the *Pchela* class appeared, roughly the same size but armed with only twin 25mm guns. They were clearly too small for the strike role and most of them were subsequently turned over to the KGB for use in patrolling the rivers and maritime frontiers of the Soviet Union.

In 1973 the first proper strike hydrofoils entered service, the 165-ton *Turya* class. Thirty were built, 123-footers armed with four 21-inch torpedo-tubes, a twin 57mm gun turret aft and a twin 25mm light automatic mounting forward. An unusual feature was a light dipping sonar on the transom stern; as there are no obvious anti-submarine weapons carried this equipment was presumably put in to allow the *Turya* class to cooperate with shore-based helicopters in hunting submarines in coastal waters.

In 1976 a new hydrofoil appeared from the Petrovsky shipyard in Leningrad and it was promptly christened the 'Sarancha' type by NATO. Only one of this class has been sighted, which suggests that she was a test-bed for the new SS-N-9 surface-to-surface missile. Four of those bulky missiles are carried in launching-tubes, two on either side of the bridge, and in addition she is protected against air attack by short-range SA-N-4 missiles and a 30mm 'Gatling' gun. Here was a formidable strike craft, with missiles capable of hitting at a range of 60 miles. The 'Sarancha' was also the first Russian craft with foils forward and aft and her combined gas turbine and diesel propulsion is credited with giving her a top speed of 45 knots.

The next class of hydrofoils, the 129ft *Matka*, started to appear two years later but reverted to the SS-N-2C, an updated variant of the 'Styx' missile. Only two missiles were carried, a reflection of the considerable weight of such weapons, and a 76mm gun forward. The single-foil system of the *Turya* design was retained, suggesting that the design actually predated that of the 'Sarancha.' Western naval opinion sees the ten *Matkas* so far

Above: The Argentinian *Intrepida* is armed with wire-guided torpedoes aft, a 40mm gun amidships and a 76mm gun forward.

completed as replacements for the older 'Osa' boats, which must be approaching the end of their useful lives.

In the last 15 years the People's Republic of China has also built military hydrofoils. The Hutong shipyard at Shanghai turned out the staggering total of 120 *Huchuan* class for the Navy, in addition to another 44 for friendly countries. It has also proved a commercial success, for 16 have been built in Rumania. The 71ft *Huchuan* is armed with twin machine guns and is driven by Russian-designed diesels at a maximum speed of 50 knots and is armed with two 21-inch torpedo-tubes.

The United States took some time to match these impressive achievements by the Communist Bloc. The experimental anti-submarine hydrofoil *High Point* (PCH-1) was completed in 1963 and reached 48 knots on two British Marine Proteus gas turbines. Her antisubmarine qualities were never fully investigated, as she spent most of her time firing Harpoon surface-to-surface missiles and other weapons. In the year that *High Point* came into service, the 328-ton *Plainview* (PCEH-1) was ordered, but she encountered mechanical setbacks and was not commissioned until 1968. She was intended to evaluate the concept of a 'hydrofoil frigate' and carried a variety of weapons during her exhaustive trials.

Both the *Plainview* and the *High Point* were experimental craft and the first intended for operational duties were a pair of prototypes, the Grumman-built *Flagstaff* (PGH-1) and Boeing's *Tucumcari* (PGH-2), which were completed in 1968. Both craft undertook a number of demonstrations around the world, *Tucumcari* going to Europe after a brief trip to Vietnam, while

Flagstaff made such an impression on the Israelis that they ordered the *Flagstaff II* design for their Coastguard.

The *Tucumcari* made an outstanding impression on her European tour and out of this stemmed the 'NATO Patrol Hydrofoil' (PHM) project. This called for 30 advanced naval strike craft to be built jointly by the United States, West Germany and Italy, and it was hoped to use an international weapons-fit. It was an ambitious plan, possibly too ambitious, for in an era of rapid inflation of costs, rising fuel bills and a general

Above: The Saudi Navy's *As Siddiq* en route through the Great Lakes from Sturgeon Bay, Wisconsin.

shortage of defence funds, a missile-armed hydrofoil was felt by many to be an expensive luxury.

In spite of mounting criticism *PHM-1* and *PHM-2* were ordered from Boeing in March 1973, but in August 1975 Congress ordered work on PHM-2 to be suspended. This immediately brought a halt to the NATO PHM programme as well and West Germany abandoned all ideas of building a missile hydrofoil. Italy, on the other hand, felt justified in continuing work to recover the investment already made and a license was taken out to build a slightly enlarged edition of the *Tucumcari* as a prototype for further development. This craft, the *Sparviero*, appeared in 1974 and showed such promise that six more were promptly

Below: Although the US Navy turned its back on FPBs after 1945, the need for inshore craft in Vietnam led to a revival. These 'Nasty' Class boats were bought from Norway.

Above: The Ecuadorean FPB *Quito*, built by Lürssen, is armed with French Exocet missiles.
Right: The Turkish 'Kartal' Class FPBs are armed with Norwegian Penguin missiles aft and two 40mm guns.

ordered. She carries an exceptionally heavy armament for an 80ft craft: two Otomat missiles aft and a 76mm gun forward.

Meanwhile Boeing were permitted to complete *PHM-1*, named *Pegasus*, and she made her first foil-borne trip in February 1975. Since then she has come through every type of trial and test imaginable and has even survived running aground in 1979. She is an impressive craft, 145ft long (with the forward foil retracted) and capable of 48 knots. She is armed with the Italian OTO-Melara 76mm Compact gun and Dutch WM-28 fire-control radar intended for the NATO PHM, and carries eight Harpoon anti-ship missiles aft (only four were mounted during early trials).

The continuing success of the trials with *Pegasus* convinced the doubters and in August 1977 Congress 'unfroze' the funds to complete the PHM program. The change of heart was too late to save *PHM-2*, named *Hercules*; her hull was scrapped and a new one started with the same name and hull-number. The first of the new PHMs to be commissioned is the *Taurus* (PHM-3) and all five are expected to be in service by 1982. Although externally similar to the *Pegasus*, the later PHMs have been completely redesigned internally to take advantage of the lessons learned since 1977.

The results of experience in *Pegasus* make interesting reading. She began her 'shakedown' in April 1977 and two months later she completed her acceptance trials, before commissioning

formally on 9 July. During the next seven months she accumulated nearly 700 hours of running under way, with 262 of those foilborne, a distance of nearly 16,000 miles. This distance compares favorably with US Navy destroyers, which log an average of about 14,000 miles each year. She is fitted with an automatic control system, which provides dynamic control during takeoff, running on the foils and 'landing' or returning to the hullborne state. In addition to stabilizing against the roll, the system controls the height of the hull above the surface of the water and all but eliminates the effect of waves. Foilborne turns are 'banked,' reducing violent motion and further improving the conditions on board. The big submerged foils also act like fixed-fin stabilizers and, if the weather becomes too severe, the commanding officer can always 'land' and turn his vessel back into a conventional 235-ton patrol craft.

As each PHM is completed she is sent to Key West, Florida, where a new PHM Squadron Two was formed in October 1981. There they will be supported by a fleet of mobile logistic support vehicles, allowing them to be independent of major base facilities. It is hoped that they will require no more than a ten-week docking and overhaul every two years, a great improvement over what was previously possible. It is intended to try PHM-RON TWO out in the Caribbean and possibly in the Mediterranean, two operating areas which favor the hit-and-run tactics of a missile-armed PHM. Although there is no reason why the PHMs should not sail across the Atlantic in company, with stops for refuelling in mid-ocean, they are more likely to be towed or carried on board a large merchant ship.

The tactics are still in their infancy, but there are many options open when five or six PHMs are in commission. One way is to use them as part of a larger battle group, with the primary intention of multiplying the number of missile-launching platforms. In this role the PHM's small radar-profile and high speed makes her a difficult target and yet she has the same missile-capability as a much larger ship. The secondary role being looked at is that of controlling 'choke points,' or in other words, ambushing hostile forces trying to push their way through relatively narrow bodies of water such as a strait between two land masses. The PHMs could work with aircraft

Above: The Norwegian FPBs *Glimt* (P.962) and *Gribb* (P.997) tied up alongside.

or by themselves, providing surveillance and a measure of deterrence as well. The high speed of the PHM is particularly valuable when it becomes necessary to investigate suspicious echoes among a large number of friendly ships, as it will enable a large area of water to be patrolled.

While the hydrofoil continues to make such strides it is easy to forget that the conventional displacement-hull FPB is still developing. Modern experience shows that the speed of an FPB has relatively little impact on her efficiency in battle; the difference between 35 and 40 knots will not affect the outcome, especially when speed falls off drastically in rough weather.

What matters is the ability of an FPB to make use of tactical information and to use her weaponry to maximum effect on the basis of that information. This means that precious weight and between-decks space must be given over to equipment for handling communications and target-plotting. Last but not

56

least, space must be found for generators to power all this equipment. Microminiaturization of electronics has done much to shrink the volume of equipment and there are now 'mini-combat systems' designed specifically for FPBs, capable of presenting the bewildering amount of raw information electronically. Only electronics can provide a speed of response capable of matching a missile travelling at the speed of sound and only electronics can provide a coordinated response to an attack – alerting the commanding officer and at the same time initiating a response, such as the launch of chaff and infra-red decoys, all in one movement.

Another problem is the long range of the latest series of missiles. The Harpoon ranges out to 60km, the MM-40 to 70km, and the Otomat to 150km, and although their manufacturers claim that they can function over the horizon just as efficiently as they do out to horizon-range, there are practical difficulties. At extreme range the target can very easily move out of the 'range gate' after the missile has been launched.

If the missile uses active radar to 'home' onto the target, that radar must be given a wider area to scan in order to pick up the target. If it is a 'fire-and-forget' missile, the triangulation of the relative position of the firing ship and the target becomes even more tricky. At extreme range it is also easier for the target to make use of countermeasures such as chaff and jamming, for the firing ship is too far away to be able to 'see' on radar the correct state of affairs.

The simple solution to these problems is to provide extra data for the missile in flight; the problem is where to get this additional information. The easiest way is to put a radar into a helicopter, which can then relay information back to the FPB,

Left: Soviet 'Stenka' Class boats at sea.
Above right: Captain and lookout on the bridge of a Soviet FPB.
With a vast coastline to protect the Soviet Navy has large numbers of FPBs, hydrofoils and small patrol craft.
Below: Music-loving Soviet sailors on the quarterdeck of a Soviet FPB.
Below right: The first of a new class of 84-foot hydrofoils built for Israel, ready for launching at Lantana, Florida.

The 56-meter Greek FPB *Antiploiarhos Laskos* was built by the French
company Constructions Mecaniques de Normandie.

or update the individual missiles in mid-flight. In 1979 Ecuador announced that she would buy the French MM-40 missile for installation in six 660-ton corvettes, and that these would each carry a light helicopter. These *Esmeraldas* class are basically enlarged patrol boats, 204ft long and driven by four-shaft diesels at a top speed of 34 knots. There is no hangar and the helicopter will be lashed down to the small flight deck right aft and this is where the problems begin. Landing a helicopter on a small platform is tricky even in a calm sea, but when the weather is rough the platform is heaving and pitching and the risks multiply. Another problem is that most small helicopters are not suited to the task of operating a sophisticated surveillance radar and passing that information back to a warship or a missile; the power required imposes a considerable load on the generators and every extra pound of gear eats into the helicopter's flying time. Helicopters are notoriously difficult to keep flying – 14 hours of maintenance to one hour of flying time is not uncommon. Their light alloy fuselages are very susceptible to corrosion from salt water and ideally they should be kept under cover for as long as possible.

Whatever the drawbacks of operating helicopters from small craft, the benefits they offer in combat make them indispensable. The new improved version of the Israeli *Saar* class, the 202ft *Alia*, has a hangar amidships, accomodating a Kiowa helicopter. A much larger class of corvettes, 253ft long and displacing 850 tons, will also have a hangar and flight deck, and it has been suggested that their role will be to provide targeting information for the Harpoon missiles which have been retrofitted to the *Reshef* class.

The fast patrol boat, having made its reputation by being small and hard to detect, is now succumbing to that fatal tendency of warships to grow in size. We have seen hulls grow steadily from 220 tons and 147ft in length only ten years ago to nearly 500 tons and over 200ft long today. Such growth is inevitable, for the inherent drawback of the small craft is that its ability to accomodate weapons is much greater than its ability to control them. Modern technology has done a lot to narrow this gap, but at the same time the performance of weapons has been improving steadily and so the gap is virtually impossible to bridge. We can only guess at what the future holds, but many more FPBs of various types will continue to be built, having made themselves a major influence on tactics and strategy.

Sadly there is little permanent record of the thousands of fast strike craft which served in the two world wars. By their very nature they tend to be ephemeral, quickly built and quickly discarded. Wooden hulls tend to rot away the aluminum alloy corrodes very easily and yet there are a surprising number of craft around, for it is at least possible to lift small craft out of the water. One or two wartime MGBs and MTBs have been preserved as war memorials in the Soviet Union, for example, and two CMBs, the 40ft *CMB.4* and the 70ft *CMB.103* survive in Great Britain.

Canada has preserved the experimental hydrofoil *Bras d'Or*, for not for any sentimental reasons. She ran very successful trials in 1969–70 but proved so costly that she was laid up in the dockyard at Halifax, Nova Scotia. There she remains, a forlorn reminder that too giant a stride can be made; it is little use achieving a technical breakthrough which does not make economic sense.

Hundreds of wartime MTBs, MGBs and motor launches survive on both sides of the Atlantic as houseboats. A walk around most backwaters will reveal the unmistakeable lines of a Vosper 70-footer or an Elco PT-Boat. It is a poor tribute to their achievements.

Right: The US Navy's patrol hydrofoil *Pegasus* (PHM.1) at high speed.
Below: The camera's wide angle lens exaggerates the size of the forward foil on the new PHM *Aries*.

Above: A Norwegian 'Storm' Class FPB fires a Penguin missile.
Below: The US Navy's *Pegasus* on trials in Puget Sound in 1977.
Only four Harpoon missiles are on board, the fifth cannister being a
dummy weighted to compensate.

Above: These Norwegian FPBs are armed with small Penguin infra-red homing missile.

INDEX

*Page numbers in italics
refer to illustrations*

Acknowledgment

The author would like to thank
David Eldred, the designer,
R. Watson who compiled the
index and the following
agencies supplied the
illustrations:

Frank Abelsen: pp 55, 63
Aldo Fraccaroli: pp 27, 30, 31
**Armada Republica
Argentina:** p 52 (top)
**A/S Kongsberg
Vapenfabrikk:** pp 54–55, 62
Austrian Military Archives:
p 15
Author's Collection: p 45 (top
left)
Boeing Marine: pp 60, 61,
62–63
Cantiere Baglietto: pp 8–9,
10–11, 26–27, 28–29
Cantiere Navale Breda:
pp 50 (top)
Foto Drüppel: pp 18 (bottom
rt), 19 (top)
Grumman: p 57 (bottom)
Imperial War Museum: pp 18
(bottom left), 19 (bottom two),
20 (top two), 20–21, 21 (top rt),
22–23, 25 (top)
Lürssenwerf: pp 50–51, 54
Ministry of Defence, London:
pp 42–43, 44
Naval Photographic Club:
pp 43, 45 (bottom), 47 (top rt)
Novosti: p 51
GA Osbon: pp 45 (top rt),
47 (top left)
Real photographs: pp 24 (top),
24–25
Science Museum, London:
pp 6–7
TASS: pp 56, 57 (top)
**Ufficio Storica della Marina
Militare:** pp 8, 12
US Navy: pp 16–17, 32, 32–33,
34, 35, 36–37, 38–39, 40–41, 44,
52–53
Vosper Thorneycroft: p 49
(top)
Vosper Ltd: p 18 (top)
William J Welch: p 53
Wright & Logan: pp 46–47,
48–49, 49 (center)